# THE LAST DAYS OF
# JUDAS ISCARIOT

**Also by Stephen Adly Guirgis**

*Our Lady of 121st Street; Jesus Hopped the A Train; In Arabia, We'd All Be Kings*

"*The Last Days of Judas Iscariot* by the phenomenally talented Stephen Adly Guirgis . . . is an extraordinary play . . . Not since Tony Kushner's *Angels in America* have I seen a play so unafraid to acknowledge the power of the spirit."

—MICHAEL BILLINGTON, *The Guardian*

"Breathtaking . . . A profoundly moving look at the difficulty of virtue and the necessity of mercy in an imperfect world."

—ELYSA GARDNER, *USA Today*

"This expressionistic fantasy draws on sound theological doctrine to advance its soul-searching meditations on guilt and redemption . . . Hearing [Guirgis's] theological arguments delivered in the rough idioms and unsophisticated accents heard on urban streets is to hear them loud and clear. In giving St. Monica the attitude of a hooker and St. Peter the voice of a dockworker, Guirgis is not diminishing their characters but attesting to their common humanity." —MARILYN STASIO, *Variety*

"One of the more scorching theatrical events of the season . . . It's almost enough to restore one's faith in the future of serious drama." —ADAM GREEN, *Vogue*

"The ambitiousness of [*The Last Days of Judas Iscariot*] represents a welcome development by the fierce urban dramatist of *Our Lady of 121st Street*. The two plays link in certain essentials: The gutter vitality of the dramatist's language is obscenely alive in the mouths of biblical folk, and Mr. Guirgis' generous heart remains with the damned." —JOHN HEILPERN, *The New York Observer*

"As compelling and complex as its subject matter."

—ROBERT DOMINGUEZ, New York *Daily News*

"*The Last Days of Judas Iscariot* is no Sunday school class . . . Depending on your faith—or lack thereof—you may find yourself disturbed or even enlightened by the arguments for and against Judas. For those whose church is the theater, there's plenty here to feed the soul." —DAVID COTE, *Time Out New York*

"Guirgis has made a name for himself as a gritty, urban writer who possesses both a natural intimacy with street language and the ability to make it sing . . . But to characterize Guirgis as a voice of the inner city might be denying his uncanny sensibility for language . . . The perennial saints and sinners who inhabit this play are given fresh and strikingly contemporary interpretations . . . The Scriptures have never read like this . . . The thousands of tiny gems within this play . . . keep the audience drinking in Guirgis' mosaic and thirsting for more."

—PETER SANTILLI, Associated Press

"[Guirgis] examines the purpose of religious faith and asks huge questions about the nature of divine love and the existence of free will." —TOBY ZINMAN, *The Philadelphia Inquirer*

"Guirgis has won friends and influenced theatergoers with a heady mixture of the sacred and the profane . . . The street smarts and cynicism of Guirgis's characters are balanced by the fact that in his plays, the church isn't merely something to ridicule or rebel against, though he does both articulately and humorously. The church can be the last refuge in a heartless, spiritually vacant world, and Guirgis derives considerable power from his unwillingness to give up on it." —ED SIEGEL, *The Boston Globe*

"Don't get the idea Guirgis is letting anyone off the hook— his nonpartisan Jesus loves Donald Rumsfeld and Osama bin Laden as much as he does Nelson Mandela."

—CHARLOTTE STOUDT, *The Village Voice*

"[A] wildly ambitious, era-melding show."

—ADA CALHOUN, *New York*

# STEPHEN ADLY GUIRGIS

# THE LAST DAYS OF JUDAS ISCARIOT

Stephen Adly Guirgis is a member of NYC's LAByrinth Theater Company. His plays have been produced on five continents and throughout the United States. They include *Our Lady of 121st Street*, which was one of ten chosen for *Best Plays of 2003* (the annual chronicle of U.S. theater) and received Best Play nominations from the Lucille Lortel Foundation, the Drama Desk, and the Outer Critics Circle; *Jesus Hopped the A Train*, which won the Edinburgh Fringe First Award, the Detroit Free Press Best Play of the Year, and the Barrymore Award, and received a Laurence Olivier nomination as London's best new play; and *In Arabia, We'd All Be Kings*, which was named one of the 10 Best of '99 by *Time Out New York*, and was a Critics Pick in *Time Out London*. All three plays were originally produced by LAByrinth and directed by Philip Seymour

Hoffman. They were published in an omnibus edition by Faber and Faber, Inc., in 2003. Guirgis was awarded a 2004 TCG fellowship, attended the 2004 Sundance Screenwriters Lab, and was named one of 2004's 25 New Faces of Independent Film by *Filmmaker* magazine. He is the recipient of new play commissions from Manhattan Theatre Club and South Coast Repertory, and is a member of New Dramatists, the Actors Studio Playwrights and Directors Unit, and the MCC Playwrights' Coalition. Television writing credits include *NYPD Blue*, *The Sopranos*, David Milch's CBS drama *Big Apple*, and Shane Salerno's NBC drama *UC: Undercover*. As an actor, he appeared in Brett C. Leonard's *Guinea Pig Solo*, produced at the Public Theater in New York, and onscreen as the born-again pedophile Joe/Earl/Bob in Todd Solondz's *Palindromes*, as well as starring opposite Michael Pitt in Brett C. Leonard's award-winning film *Jailbait* for Belladonna Pictures. He lives in New York City.

# THE LAST DAYS OF
# JUDAS ISCARIOT

## STEPHEN ADLY GUIRGIS

FARRAR, STRAUS AND GIROUX / NEW YORK

Farrar, Straus and Giroux
18 West 18th Street, New York 10011

Library of Congress Cataloging-in-Publication Data
Guirgis, Stephen Adly.
The Last days of Judas Iscariot / by Stephen Adly Guirgis.—1st ed.
    p.   cm.
    ISBN: 978-0-571-21101-2 (pbk. : alk. paper)
    1. Judas Iscariot—Drama.    2. Bible. N.T.—History of Biblical events—
Drama.    I. Title.

PS3697.U4S L37 2005
812'.5—dc22

                                                                    2005048810

*Designed by Gretchen Achilles*

www.fsgbooks.com

26  28  30  29  27  25

*In memory of Nicole duFresne*
*(1977–2005)*
*and Terrence Morris*
*(1974–2005)*
R.I.P.

# Introduction

My theater company is called LAByrinth. We go away every
summer to workshop new material and to fall in love again.
One year, they called and asked me, "What are you bringing up
this summer?" I said, "I don't know." They said, "Should we
just put you down as 'I don't know'?" I said, "I don't know."
They said, "How about we just put you down on the schedule
as 'Untitled Guirgis Project'?" I said, "Okay." And then—and I
honestly have no idea why—I said, "Put me down as *The Last
Days of Judas Iscariot*." And then I hung up the phone.

   I grew up Catholic, so the story of the play is told within
those parameters. When I was a kid, the story of Judas
troubled me a lot. It didn't make sense to me, it frightened
me, and it seemed to fly in the face of the notion of the
all-loving and all-merciful God that the very good and loving
nuns at the Corpus Christi School on 121st Street were
teaching me about. I can't remember if I raised my hand
and asked questions. I can't remember if I went home and
asked my mom about it. What I do remember is that I
stopped believing the story, and that not believing—or not
wanting to believe—made me feel a lot of things that didn't
feel good. I was nine or ten at the time. From then on—unless
I was in trouble—I was in no hurry to seek out God. In fact, I
had no sense of who or what God was. I did believe that "God"
existed—I still do—but that was about it. And knowing or
believing that God existed but avoiding him probably instilled

in me a lot of shame and guilt. There's nothing wrong with that. I wasn't avoiding "God." I was avoiding myself.

I don't want to know too much about why I write plays or why I wrote this play in particular. Perhaps it's true that the best way to move forward is to go back, and so, in writing this play, I went back. I don't know. I do know that I am in continuous need of the Spiritual and that I usually go to great lengths to avoid it. And I think I'm not alone in that. And I think a connection to the Spiritual is essential to us as individuals and to the world as a whole. I think our survival depends on it. I also think that religion gets a bad rap in this country and that non-maniac-type people who are religious or spiritual have a responsibility to stand up, be counted, and gently encourage others to consider matters of faith and to define for themselves what their responsibilities are and what it means to try to be "good." It's not about joining a team or a church or choosing sides or learning a prayer. It's not about man-made concepts of good and evil. It's not about doing "enough" or "too little." It's not about shame and guilt. It's about You. It's about the collective Us. Thomas Merton said, "To be a saint means to be myself." What if that were true? What is it that we need to overcome in order to truly be "Ourselves"? I won't pretend at all that this play answers that question, but if it provokes the question in you, then please let it. Ponder it. Because we need you.

—STEPHEN ADLY GUIRGIS
NEW YORK CITY, 2005

# THE LAST DAYS OF
# JUDAS ISCARIOT

**THE LAST DAYS OF JUDAS ISCARIOT** was originally produced by
the LAByrinth Theater Company (Philip Seymour Hoffman
and John Ortiz, artistic directors) and the Public Theater
(George C. Wolfe, producer, and Mara Manus, executive
director) at the Public Theater, New York, on March 2, 2005.
It was directed by Philip Seymour Hoffman; sets were designed
by Andromache Chalfant; costumes by Mimi O'Donnell;
lights by Japhy Weideman; and sound by Darron L. West.
Fight direction was by Rick Sordelet. The production stage
manager was Monica Moore. The cast was as follows:

| | |
|---|---|
| SATAN | *Eric Bogosian* |
| GLORIA/MOTHER TERESA | *Liza Colón-Zayas* |
| JUDGE/CAIAPHAS THE ELDER/ SAINT MATTHEW | *Jeffrey DeMunn* |
| LORETTA/MARY MAGDALENE/ SISTER GLENNA | *Yetta Gottesman* |
| BAILIFF/SIMON THE ZEALOT | *Salvatore Inzerillo* |
| SIGMUND FREUD/SAINT THOMAS/ SOLDIER 1 | *Adrian Martinez* |
| PONTIUS PILATE/UNCLE PINO | *Stephen McKinley Henderson* |
| MATTHIAS OF GALILEE/ SAINT PETER/SOLDIER 2 | *Craig "Mums" Grant* |
| JESUS OF NAZARETH | *John Ortiz* |
| JUDAS ISCARIOT | *Sam Rockwell* |

| | |
|---|---|
| SAINT MONICA/SOLDIER 3 | *Elizabeth Rodriguez* |
| HENRIETTA ISCARIOT | *Deborah Rush* |
| BUTCH HONEYWELL | *Kohl Sudduth* |
| FABIANA AZIZA CUNNINGHAM | *Callie Thorne* |
| YUSEF EL-FAYOUMY | *Yul Vázquez* |

# Characters

SATAN

GLORIA

MOTHER TERESA

JUDGE LITTLEFIELD

CAIAPHAS THE ELDER

SAINT MATTHEW

LORETTA

MARY MAGDALENE

BAILIFF (JULIUS OF OUTER
   MONGOLIA)

SIMON THE ZEALOT

SIGMUND FREUD

SAINT THOMAS

PONTIUS PILATE

UNCLE PINO

MATTHIAS OF GALILEE

SAINT PETER

JESUS OF NAZARETH

JUDAS ISCARIOT

SAINT MONICA

HENRIETTA ISCARIOT

SISTER GLENNA

BUTCH HONEYWELL

FABIANA AZIZA CUNNINGHAM

YUSEF EL-FAYOUMY

SOLDIERS

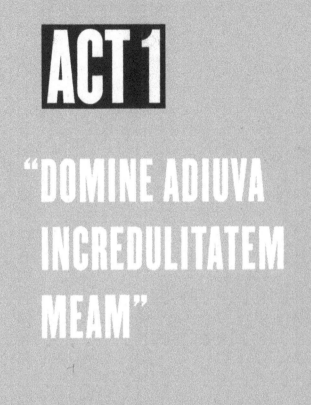

# ACT 1

## "DOMINE ADIUVA INCREDULITATEM MEAM"

*Darkness. Rain. From nowhere, a woman emerges from her past.*

HENRIETTA ISCARIOT: No parent should have to bury a
child . . . No mother should have to bury a son. Mothers
are not meant to bury sons. It is not in the natural order
of things.

I buried my son. In a potter's field. In a field of Blood.
In empty, acrid silence. There was no funeral. There were
no mourners. His friends all absent. His father dead. His
sisters refusing to attend. I discovered his body alone, I dug
his grave alone, I placed him in a hole, and covered him with
dirt and rock alone. I was not able to finish burying him
before sundown, and I'm not sure if that affected his fate . . .

I begrudge God none of this. I do not curse him or
bemoan my lot. And though my heart keeps beating only
to keep breaking—I do not question why.

I remember the morning my son was born as if it was
yesterday. The moment the midwife placed him in my
arms, I was infused with a love beyond all measure and
understanding. I remember holding my son, and looking
over at my own mother and saying, "Now I understand why
the sun comes up at day and the stars come out at night. I
understand why rain falls gently. Now I understand you,
Mother" . . .

I loved my son every day of his life, and I will love him
ferociously long after I've stopped breathing. I am a simple
woman. I am not bright or learn-ed. I do not read. I do
not write. My opinions are not solicited. My voice is not

important . . . On the day of my son's birth I was infused
with a love beyond all measure and understanding . . . The
world tells me that God is in Heaven and that my son is in
Hell. I tell the world the one true thing I know: If my son is
in Hell, then there is no Heaven—because if my son sits in
Hell, *there is no God.*

JESUS, *carrying a bucket, has approached the woman. He kisses her
cheek. She does not notice. They vanish.*

*A courtroom. Court is in session. A woman with wings,*
GLORIA, *rises.*

GLORIA:  Between Heaven and Hell—there is another place.
This place: Hope. Hope—is located right over here in
downtown Purgatory.

JUDGE LITTLEFIELD:  *Next case!*

GLORIA:  Now, Purgatory, contrary to popular belief, has
plumbing, and bodegas, and they even got a movie theater
and a little park that people can walk their dogs at. Hope—
well it ain't got none a that, and it definitely don't smell good.

JUDGE LITTLEFIELD:  *Next case, Bailiff!*

GLORIA:  I worked here in Hope for two and a half years—thass
how I got these wings. And I wouldn't trade nothing for
these wings—I can fly with these wings! At night, I fly down
to Earth, and I watch my littlest Babyboy sleep. He's seven,
and he's got a picture of me on his wall—right in between
Shaquille O'Neal and the Incredible Hulk. Then, I go fly
uptown to the window of my oldest Babygirl's house and
watch my granchild, Little Bit, sleep. Most nights I can see
my oldest Babygirl, Tanya, with her feet in a pot of hot
water, always studying books; and I'll stick around to see
her man, Winston, come home late at night from work,

always with a muffin or a hamburger for my Babygirl. Winston's love for my Babygirl is all over his face—I was wrong about him, I always thought he was shifty . . . When I get back to Heaven, I tell my husband, DeLayne, all about it. DeLayne don't like to fly, but he likes to hear the stories, and he likes how I look like when I come home from Earth all "windblown" . . . Now Hope, it changes with the times, but has stood always as God's gift to the last of his children. It is said that every civilization rearranges the cosmic furniture differently. In biblical times, Hope was an Oasis in the Desert. In medieval days, a shack free of Plague. Today, Hope is no longer a place for contemplation— litigation being the preferred new order of the day.

JUDGE LITTLEFIELD: *Where's my damn bailiff??!!*

BAILIFF: Here, sir.

JUDGE LITTLEFIELD: *Then call the next damn case!!!*

BAILIFF: Yes, sir. *"God and the Kingdom of Heaven and Earth versus Thorseen the Implacable: Motion to appeal"!*

JUDGE LITTLEFIELD: *Denied—Next case!*

BAILIFF: *"God and the Kingdom of Heaven and Earth versus Henry Wayne Masters—"*

JUDGE LITTLEFIELD: *Nope!*

BAILIFF: *"God and the Kingdom of Heaven and Earth versus Benedict Arnold—"*

JUDGE LITTLEFIELD: *Aw, hell, no!*

BAILIFF: *"God and the Kingdom of Heaven and Earth versus Judas Iscariot—"*

JUDGE LITTLEFIELD: *—"Judas Iscariot" ??!! Who brings this crap before me??!!*

CUNNINGHAM: Your Honor, my name is Fabiana Aziza Cunningham—

JUDGE LITTLEFIELD: —Never heard of you!

CUNNINGHAM: I live in Purgatory.

JUDGE LITTLEFIELD: Well you shoulda kept your legs closed! *Motion denied! Next case!*

CUNNINGHAM: Your Honor, I have a writ signed by Saint Peter at the Gates of Heaven!

JUDGE LITTLEFIELD: *Next case!*

CUNNINGHAM: But I have a writ!

BAILIFF: She has a writ, sir.

JUDGE LITTLEFIELD: Excuse me?!

BAILIFF: Just saying: The lady, she's got a writ, so, I mean—

JUDGE LITTLEFIELD: —Bailiff: let's set up a little *signal* between the two of us, okay?

BAILIFF: Okay.

JUDGE LITTLEFIELD: Good. Now, when I come to court dressed as Ethel Merman in a one-piece bathing suit, that'll be my *signal* to you that I want your *opinion!*

BAILIFF: Yes, sir.

JUDGE LITTLEFIELD: *Next case!!*

BAILIFF: But what about the writ, sir?

JUDGE LITTLEFIELD: What's your name, Bailiff?!

BAILIFF: Julius of Outer Mongolia.

JUDGE LITTLEFIELD: You're on work-release from Purgatory, Julius—correct?

BAILIFF: Yes, sir.

JUDGE LITTLEFIELD: Wanna get to Heaven someday? Eat fried chicken and mashed potatoes, feel the sun on your face.

BAILIFF: Very much, sir.

JUDGE LITTLEFIELD: *Then call the next damn case!!!*

BAILIFF: Yes, sir. Absolutely, sir.

JUDGE LITTLEFIELD: Good. Have a lollipop.

BAILIFF: Thank you, sir.

JUDGE LITTLEFIELD: Next case!

BAILIFF: But, like, the writ, sir—

JUDGE LITTLEFIELD: *Bailiff!!!!!!!!*

YUSEF AKBAR WAHID AL-NASSAR GAMEL EL-FAYOUMY *rises dramatically from his seat in the courtroom.*

EL-FAYOUMY: Your Honor, if I may?!

JUDGE LITTLEFIELD: Who speaks before me?!

EL-FAYOUMY: It is I, Yusef Akbar Wahid Al-Nassar Gamel El-Fayoumy!

JUDGE LITTLEFIELD: *Who the hell are you?!*

EL-FAYOUMY: An attorney, great sir! Willing and able to prosecute this sham of a case and defend the Gates of Heaven and the Kingdom of God against this big shenanigan of a so-called writ, great handsome sir! Look no further, Your Honor! Yusef Akbar Wahid Al-Nassar Gamel El-Fayoumy is a *beacon* for justice!

JUDGE LITTLEFIELD: A "beacon," eh?

EL-FAYOUMY: May I approach you?

JUDGE LITTLEFIELD: *The bench, not me!*

EL-FAYOUMY: The bench! Of course! YES!—And it is a lovely bench, splendid and sturdy like the great derrière that rests upon it!! Your Honor, I received wind of this so-called "writ" several weeks ago. I have been preparing night and day to refute the allegations it contains!

CUNNINGHAM: Your Honor, let the record reflect I have no opposition to Mr. El-Fayoumy here.

JUDGE LITTLEFIELD (*to* CUNNINGHAM): *Speak when spoken to!!!*

EL-FAYOUMY: Do not bait this great man, lady! He presided over the appeal of Attila the Hun when you were nothing more than a cheap shot of whiskey on your great-great-grandfather's first unpaid bar tab!

JUDGE LITTLEFIELD: Well said!

EL-FAYOUMY: Forgive the outburst.

JUDGE LITTLEFIELD: . . . You got a license to practice, Mr. El-Fajita?

EL-FAYOUMY: A license? A license! Yes. Absolutely!! Submitted for your most scrupulously discerning approval, eminently great sir!

EL-FAYOUMY *crosses, fumbles, searching his pockets for the license.*

BAILIFF (*cautiously*): Sir, his name's El-Fa*youmy*.
JUDGE LITTLEFIELD: What?
BAILIFF: You called him El-Fajita.
JUDGE LITTLEFIELD: Just gimme my glasses!
BAILIFF: You're wearing them, sir.
JUDGE LITTLEFIELD (*exploding*): My *other* glasses!!!!!!!!!
BAILIFF: Oh. Here.
EL-FAYOUMY: Most worshipful lord and master: very tiny problem. My license, I seem to have left it in my other suit. I could rush back to Hell and retrieve it—
JUDGE LITTLEFIELD: From Hell are you?
EL-FAYOUMY: Temporarily detained—a problem with my papers.
JUDGE LITTLEFIELD: You sure about that?
EL-FAYOUMY: Quite sure, your grace. I attribute the mix-up to the Americanization of the afterlife—completely understandable in lieu of recent events.
JUDGE LITTLEFIELD: You're damn right.
EL-FAYOUMY: Yes, your eminence—as are you, great sir!
JUDGE LITTLEFIELD: Cunningham! Let me see this "writ."
CUNNINGHAM: Here, Your Honor.

JUDGE *reads the writ.*

EL-FAYOUMY (*an aside*): You have great legs, Fabiana. Free for dinner, perhaps?
JUDGE LITTLEFIELD: Cunningham! This writ is garbage! *Next case!*

CUNNINGHAM: Your Honor, my client—

JUDGE LITTLEFIELD: Your client is Judas Iscariot! Your client sold out the son of God, for Chrissakes!

CUNNINGHAM: Your Honor, that has no bearing—

JUDGE LITTLEFIELD: Cunningham—Judas Iscariot committed the one unforgivable sin. Everybody knows it—

EL-FAYOUMY: —The sin of despair!

JUDGE LITTLEFIELD: And then he did the world a favor and hung himself!

EL-FAYOUMY: From the olive branch, the coward!

JUDGE LITTLEFIELD: Next case!!

CUNNINGHAM: Your Honor, that writ you hold in your hand is signed by Saint Peter!

JUDGE LITTLEFIELD: I know Peter, and he's prone to error, believe me. And he's rash—

EL-FAYOUMY: Rash! Absolutely! A little place called the Garden of Gethsemane ring a bell, Fabiana? When the authorities came to arrest Jesus—after *your client* sold him out with a kiss—what did Peter do?

CUNNINGHAM: I know what he did.

EL-FAYOUMY: *Well, know it again!!* Peter took out his sword and started chopping off the ears of the authority! Can you imagine?! Jesus had to correct him, put the ears back on—it was a big mess, really.

JUDGE LITTLEFIELD: Next case!

CUNNINGHAM: But Your Honor—

JUDGE LITTLEFIELD: Next case!!

EL-FAYOUMY: Come Fabiana: dinner and a sensual massage—it will soothe you—

CUNNINGHAM: —Your Honor, I cite the Beatitudes, and Kierkegaard. I cite Christ on the Cross!

JUDGE LITTLEFIELD: I cite my foot in your ass, Cunningham!

CUNNINGHAM: I cite Hegel: Within every idea—*thesis*—is

contained its contradiction—*antithesis*—and out of that
struggle is created—*synthesis*. Synthesis, Your Honor! The
Union of Opposites—their interdependence and their
inevitable clash producing what's next—what must be
revealed: God's Perfect Love versus God's Rightful Justice
equals what, Your Honor?

JUDGE LITTLEFIELD: *Out of my courtroom!!!*

CUNNINGHAM: The synthesis of Love and Justice can produce
only Mercy and Forgiveness, Your Honor! If a just God sits
in Heaven, it can fall no other way!

JUDGE LITTLEFIELD: Next case!

CUNNINGHAM: But Your Honor—

JUDGE LITTLEFIELD: *Next case! NEXT CASE NEXT CASE
NEXT CASE!!!!!*

*The gavel bangs. Blackout.*

JUDGE LITTLEFIELD (*sotto voce*): Crazy Mick Bitch.

*In darkness, we hear voices, noises, and portentous rumblings like
an earthquake. Lights flash.*

VOICE OF ASSISTANT STAGE MANAGER: All right now, people!—
Cue them trumpets and the dancing camels!

*The sounds of trumpets and dancing camels are heard. Music
and wild lights.*

SAINT MONICA: Thanks, boys!
        Hey, y'all. Welcome to my world . . . So this is the
part of the story, where, if it wasn't for me, there wouldn't
be no more parts to the fuckin' story, okay? My name is
MONICA—better known to you mere mortals as SAINT

Monica. Yeah, dass right, SAINT—as in "better not don't get up in *my* grill 'cuz I'll mess your shit up, 'cuz I'm a Saint and I got mad saintly connects," okay? You ever drove down Santa Monica Boulevard? You ever ate some sushis down the Santa Monica Pier? Well dass *my* boulevard and *my* pier, and dass all I gotta say about that—word to the wise, word is most definitely B-O-N-D bond . . . Anyways (lemme catch my breaf). Anyways, up in Heaven, a lotta peoples don't wanna hang with me 'cuz they say I'm a Nag. It's true. And you know what I say about that? I say: "Fuck them bitches," 'cuz—you know what—I *am* a Nag, and if I wasn't a Nag, I wouldn't never made it to be no Saint, and the church wouldn't a had no Father of the Church named Saint Augustine—'cuz I birthed the mothahfuckah, raised him, and when he started messin' up, like, all the time and constantly, I nagged God's ass to save him! I nagged and nagged and nagged and nagged till God got so tired of my shit that he did save my son, and my son—Saint Augustine— he stopped bangin' whores and sippin' on some wine and he became learn-ed, so fuckin' learn-ed that he's known as one of the Fathers of the Church, and you could look that shit up! Go ahead, look it up right now, I'll wait! . . . Dass right: "Father Up In This Mothahfuckah"! "Father of the Church"—got a plaque and everything! So if I hadn't been a Nag, All a Y'all niggas woulda been a bastard church, so, sip on dat, bitches! . . . Anyways (lemme catch my breaf), okay: As a result of my reputation of having God's ear, a lotta mothahfuckahs pray to me—I have three full-time assistants just to sift through it all. Long story short, I was axed to look into the case of Judas Iscariot by this Irish Gypsy lawyer bitch in Purgatory named Cunningham. She wanted me to do some naggin' to God on Judas's behalf, and, quite frankly, I was impressed by *her* nagging abilities—'cuz that bitch nagged my ass day and night for forty days . . . But I don't nag for juss any anybody, and I definitely don't nag for no mothahfuckah I don't know, so, I went down to check out Judas for my own self—

*And now she is with* JUDAS.

(*To audience*): He looked fuckin' retarded, he wouldn't talk or nuthin'. He didn't seem to hear me, and I'm not someone who has a problem expressing myself. I figured he was fakin', so I did this:
(*To* JUDAS): Yo, Judas! . . . Judas! . . . Yo, You Deaf, mothahfuckah? . . . Judas, yo! . . .
(*To audience*): I smacked the bitch around a little.

MONICA *slaps, kicks, shoves.*

　　Yo, Helen Keller! Yo, wake up! . . . Don't front—I know you could hear me . . .
(*To audience*): Then I started snappin' on his ass.
(*To* JUDAS): Yo, Judas, you got change for thirty pieces of silver, mothahfuckah?! . . . Yo, Judas, how much you pay for that haircut?—thirty pieces of silver?! Yo Judas, why you so "hung" up? C'mon, let's "hang" out. C'mon, bitch, go out on a "limb"! You want a "olive"? C'mon mothahfuckah, have a "olive." Wanna go to the "Olive Garden" restaurant? Day got good "Olive Oil" there . . . Ah-aight, fine, come on, Judas, whaddya say you an' me go down to the bar and—betray some mothahfuckahs! Whaddya say?! I know you like betraying! What's up, you ain't in the mood to betray today?! Ah-aight, mothahfuckah, we can just "hang"?! Get it? Hang?! Get it?! Do you get it?! . . . Wassamatter?! Hungry?! How 'bout some

supper?! You want some supper, mothahfuckah?! C'mon, one last supper, whaddya say?!

(*To audience*): I couldn't break him. So I sat down next to him.

*She sits.*

I sat with Judas Iscariot for three days. Then, on the night of the third day, sumpthin' happened. While I was restin' my vocal chords, I saw sumpthin' unexpected. I saw a single tear fall out Judas's eye. Just one. When the tear hit the ground, I saw it was red like a ruby. I looked into his eyes, like this:

*She looks into* JUDAS's *eyes.*

He couldn't look at me. Or he looked through me. I couldn't tell. His eyes was empty. He barely breathed. He was like a catatonic statue of a former human being. And I detected sadness in him. Paralyzing, immobilizing, overwhelming sadness. His sadness ran through him like a river that had frozen up and died and no one lived there no more. After a while, I didn't know what else to do, so I thought I'd just hold him in my arms for like a minute, warm him up before I left.

*She cradles* JUDAS *in her arms. Beat.*

I held him in my arms for four days. On the third day, I remembered how Jesus had said that God has the biggest love for the least of his creatures—and Judas was the leastest creature I had ever seen. On the fourth day, Judas dropped another single tear. It was clear-colored this time and it evaporated into the earth on impact. He trembled briefly, then froze up again . . . I had seen enough. I took off my outer garments and left them for him so he could smell something human. I collected my tears in a bucket and poured it on his face so he could taste the salt. Then I went back home and got on the horn to God. I dialed direct, yo. Some people call it being a Nag, I call it doing my Job. I got a calling, y'all—you should try giving me a shout if ya ever need it, 'cuz my name is Saint Monica, I'm the mother of Saint Augustine, one of the Fathers of the Church, and ya know what? My ass gets results!

*A gavel bangs.*

JUDGE LITTLEFIELD: *Next case!*
BAILIFF: *"God and the Kingdom of Heaven and Earth versus Judas Iscariot"!*
JUDGE LITTLEFIELD: Bailiff!!!!!
BAILIFF: She got a writ signed by God, sir.
SAINT MONICA: *Signed, Sealed, Delivered, mothahfuckah! Peace!!*
CUNNINGHAM: Here is the writ, Your Honor—note the signature at the bottom.

SAINT MONICA *and* JUDAS *vanish.*

JUDGE LITTLEFIELD: Bailiff!! Bailiff!! Where's El-Fajita?

EL-FAYOUMY *rises with panache.*

EL-FAYOUMY: Present and accounted for and dripping with anticipation to defend with marvelous cunning and great relish the Kingdom of Heaven and Earth and your great sir-ness against the Satan-spawned traitor Judas Iscariot and

his beguiling but outlandishly misguided counsel, most
eminently great and rakishly handsome great sir!!!

*Beat.*

JUDGE LITTLEFIELD (*re: the writ*): Cunningham, I do not like it
when lawyers go over my head.
CUNNINGHAM: You gave me no choice.
EL-FAYOUMY: *Objection, Your Honor!!!* As human beings, we
always have choice! Motion to strike!
JUDGE LITTLEFIELD: Mr. El-Fajita, you are aware that the trial
hasn't actually begun yet, right?
EL-FAYOUMY: Uh . . . Yes . . . Right. Of course. I was merely,
uh . . . Yes, sir . . .

EL-FAYOUMY *sheepishly sits.*

JUDGE LITTLEFIELD: "Fabiana" "Aziza" "Cunningham," that
right?
CUNNINGHAM: It is.
JUDGE LITTLEFIELD: So where's the red hair and freckles,
Cunningham?
CUNNINGHAM: My mother was a Romanian Gypsy who settled
in Vinegar Hill in Harlem in the 1960s.
JUDGE LITTLEFIELD: And your father?
CUNNINGHAM: A local parish priest.
JUDGE LITTLEFIELD: Got more than his palm read, did he? All
right, then, Cunningham, I think it only fair at this juncture
to tell you some things about myself, things that may,
perhaps, inspire you to take your little mission elsewhere.
For example, I strongly dislike Tapioca Pudding—
EL-FAYOUMY (*rising*): Tapioca, the worst, I spit on it!

JUDGE LITTLEFIELD: Siddown!!

(*to* CUNNINGHAM): But even more than Tapioca, Cunningham, I dislike the following: Defense Attorneys as a rule, half-breeds in general, and Judas Iscariot as anything other than a cautionary tale. Now that a problem for you? ·

CUNNINGHAM: No.

JUDGE LITTLEFIELD: You ever met God, Cunningham?

CUNNINGHAM: I don't know that I believe in God.

JUDGE LITTLEFIELD: You've just handed me a writ signed by Him, and, yet, you don't know if you believe?

CUNNINGHAM: Correct.

JUDGE LITTLEFIELD: Well, what if God appeared to you, Cunningham? Just one day, boom! God: White Beard, Flowing Robe, The Whole Rack a Lamb.

CUNNINGHAM: Your Honor—

JUDGE LITTLEFIELD: What if you were to go home tonight, Cunningham, and Jesus Christ himself were to greet you at your door with a dozen Krispy Kremes and a quart of cold milk and say: "Cunningham. Fabiana. It's me. I really am that thing that you've always feared more than doubted"—what would you do?

CUNNINGHAM: Your Honor—

JUDGE LITTLEFIELD: And what if you let him in, Cunningham, and you sat down with The Man for just, say, three minutes? And you could touch him and inspect him and interrogate him all you want and have him do miracles and tell you the exact story of your life, and you ended up convinced—convinced, Cunningham—wiping away tears of joy and relief on your living-room couch. If he *proved* it to you, Cunningham, would you believe then?

CUNNINGHAM: If he proved it, I suppose I would have to.

JUDGE LITTLEFIELD: After only three minutes?

CUNNINGHAM: But that would never happen—

STEPHEN ADLY GUIRGIS

JUDGE LITTLEFIELD: Cunningham, you're the cynical, faithless spawn of a Crackpot Gypsy and a Defrocked Mick—yet you just told me Jesus would have you on your knees in three minutes.

CUNNINGHAM: So?

JUDGE LITTLEFIELD: So consider this: Your friend Judas? He had Jesus for three *years*! Think about that, Cunningham. Three years in the foxhole with the best friend ya ever had, then he shot him in the back for a pack of Kools. Think what that says about the essential character of the man. Now go home and stir *that* into your wee Gypsy teapot! *Petition's invalid, Motion denied! Next case!*

EL-FAYOUMY: Pure genius! I am erect!

CUNNINGHAM: Your Honor, this petition is signed by *God!*

JUDGE LITTLEFIELD: Yeah, but it ain't signed by your client, now, is it?

CUNNINGHAM: My client is catatonic, he's incapable of signing.

JUDGE LITTLEFIELD: If he's catatonic, then how do you know he wants an appeal in the first place?

CUNNINGHAM: Who couldn't want to appeal "eternal damnation"?

JUDGE LITTLEFIELD: Someone who was aware of his own self-inflicted erosion of the capacity to be filled by Grace . . . Someone too prideful to ask for forgiveness even in the face of the fiery furnace. Or maybe, he don't bother askin', 'cuz he knows he don't deserve it!

CUNNINGHAM: Your Honor, the only person who *needs* forgiveness is the one who doesn't deserve it.

JUDGE LITTLEFIELD: Then let him ask!

CUNNINGHAM: I'm asking for him!

JUDGE LITTLEFIELD: *Out of my courtroom, sister, and may God have mercy on your blasted arrogant soul!* Now get thee back Uptown, woman. Stop your rabble-rousing, and get humble—'cuz you ain't gonna get to Heaven by trying to dismantle the Natural Order of Things that the good lord has so thoughtfully put together!!!

CUNNINGHAM: Your Honor, are you a citizen of Heaven?

JUDGE LITTLEFIELD: Bailiff! Remove this woman!

CUNNINGHAM: You live here with us—you know no more about God's Law than anyone else in this court!

JUDGE LITTLEFIELD: My papers are pending—I'll be up there any day now.

CUNNINGHAM: Your papers have been pending since 1864, Your Honor, that's a hundred and forty years—

JUDGE LITTLEFIELD: —If there's an insinuation at the end of that statement, Cunningham, I suggest you don't make it!

CUNNINGHAM: Not an insinuation, Your Honor, but a question: If the "truth" really does set us free, then what is it, Your Honor, that is progressively precluding your capacity to respond to the call of that truth? Because "a hundred and forty years" suggests to me that you are moving not closer, but farther and farther away from it every day!

JUDGE LITTLEFIELD: What the hell does "Judas Iscariot" have to do with my truth, Cunningham? I didn't hang myself from some olive branch!

CUNNINGHAM: Not from an olive branch, but on a battlefield in northern Georgia in 1864. Allatoona. And the tree—Oak, I believe. Your Honor, I have to wonder what your honest answer will be, when you are someday asked how different you are now from that day when you died?

*An uncomfortable pause.*

JUDGE LITTLEFIELD: . . . Tomorrow morning. Nine a.m. That work for you?

CUNNINGHAM: It does.

JUDGE LITTLEFIELD (*to* BAILIFF): Put it on the docket.

BAILIFF: Docket?

JUDGE LITTLEFIELD: Just write it down!

BAILIFF: Um . . .

BAILIFF *takes out a pen and scribbles on his hand.*

JUDGE LITTLEFIELD: Anything else, Fabiana Aziza
   Cunningham?

CUNNINGHAM: No, Your Honor.

JUDGE LITTLEFIELD: *Next fuckin' Case!!!!!!!*

EL-FAYOUMY: Fear not, your grace, I shall slay this fallen
   woman as the crocodile slays the one-legged newt!

JUDGE LITTLEFIELD: *NEXT CASE NEXT CASE NEXT CASE
   NEXT CASE!!*

*The gavel bangs.* GLORIA *and* LORETTA, *wearing a hospital gown,
appear.*

GLORIA: Very little is actually known about Judas Iscariot—
   Oh! this is my fellow jury member Loretta. On earth, she's
   currently on Life Support.

LORETTA: Hi, Hello!

GLORIA: Have they figured out whether you comin' or goin' yet?

LORETTA: Not really. "Any day now," they say.

GLORIA *takes a peek around.*

GLORIA (*conspiratorially*): Say, Loretta—you smoke cigarettes?

LORETTA: Well, not unconscious on a respirator.

GLORIA: Yeah but—you got one for me?

LORETTA: Maybe in my clutch. Oh. Here.

LORETTA *produces a cigarette.*

GLORIA: Oh snap—Newports?! Oh, you my girl now! You got
 a light?
LORETTA (*producing a lighter*): It's a NASCAR lighter.
GLORIA (*uninterested*): Mmmm-hmmm.

*She lights her cigarette, inhales.*

(*To audience*): So anyways—about Judas, not a lot is known
 except that he was chosen to be an Apostle, he betrayed
 Jesus, and then he hung his-self. Not a lot to go on—
 especially when we're meant to rely on facts.
LORETTA: You know, I had an uncle—can I say this?
GLORIA: Go ahead.
LORETTA (*addressing the audience*): When I was a little girl, my
 drunk uncle Pino, he used to like to go around saying:

UNCLE PINO *appears.*

UNCLE PINO: "I believe, because it is absurd! It is certain
 because it is impossible!"

UNCLE PINO *vanishes.*

GLORIA: What did he mean by that?
LORETTA: No clue . . . But I think—

BUTCH HONEYWELL *enters.*

BUTCH HONEYWELL: Ladies, we're back.
GLORIA (*to audience*): Oh wait—hold up!

GLORIA *snaps her fingers dramatically and both* BUTCH *and* LORETTA *freeze in time.*

Now that's Butch Honeywell: and unlike Loretta, he definitely dead. And also unlike Loretta, he got no real interest in finding that out.

GLORIA *snaps her fingers again and* BUTCH *and* LORETTA *unfreeze.*

So Butch, did we miss anything in there?

BUTCH HONEYWELL: Oh, just some crap about the essential paradox of man: How we refuse to juxtapose the absolute to the relative, and some other some-such about paradox as an ontological definition which expresses the relation between an existing cognitive spirit and eternal truth— You know, bullshit.
Listen, they passed out the lunch menus—I ordered you guys the Combo Club with Fritters.

LORETTA: Fritters: awesome! Thanks, Butch.

BUTCH HONEYWELL: Right this way, ladies.

*The gavel bangs.*

JUDGE LITTLEFIELD: Next witness!

EL-FAYOUMY: Great Magnificent Sir! The Prosecution now calls Henrietta Iscariot, mother to Judas Iscariot, to the stand!

BAILIFF: State your name, ma'am.

HENRIETTA ISCARIOT: Henrietta Iscariot.

EL-FAYOUMY: Yes . . . Good day, Miss Iscariot.

HENRIETTA ISCARIOT: Good day.

EL-FAYOUMY: Yes . . . Well . . . I can't help but notice, Miss

Iscariot, that you are a very well-built woman—would it be fair to say "your cup runneth over"?

HENRIETTA ISCARIOT: Um, all the Iscariots are buxom, if that's what you mean?

EL-FAYOUMY: *My meaning exactly!!* Now then: can you recall if Judas Iscariot as an infant was prone to steal more than his fair share of milk from your deliciously well-apportioned bosom?

HENRIETTA ISCARIOT: I can't recall that. No.

EL-FAYOUMY: Very well, but can you recall . . . *this!!!* I take you back to the year eight. You were a single parent raising many children, Judas being your eldest, and the man of the family. You sent him out fishing to get food for you and his poor starving sisters. What happened next?

HENRIETTA ISCARIOT (*to* JUDGE LITTLEFIELD): Do I have to answer?

JUDGE LITTLEFIELD: Just tell the truth, ma'am.

HENRIETTA ISCARIOT: Well, Judas didn't come home till very late. I waited by the fire. I was worried, he was only eight. I was concerned that maybe the Romans had detained him for shoplifting again—

EL-FAYOUMY: A shoplifter! So please the court!

HENRIETTA ISCARIOT: But then he came home.

JUDAS *crosses, sits on floor. He is eight.*

JUDAS: Hi Mommy.

HENRIETTA ISCARIOT: Judas! I was so worried.

JUDAS: Look what I got, Mommy! A spinning top!

HENRIETTA ISCARIOT: Judas, did you catch any fish? Your sisters are weeping with hunger—

EL-FAYOUMY: Weeping, your great sir! Weeping and Wailing!

JUDAS: I caught five fish, Mommy!

HENRIETTA ISCARIOT: But where are they?

JUDAS: I sold them in the market and bought this spinning top. Look how it spins, Mommy!

HENRIETTA ISCARIOT: Judas Iscariot, I am ashamed of you!

JUDAS: But Mommy—

HENRIETTA ISCARIOT: —*Selfish boy, you will come to no good!!!*

EL-FAYOUMY: *"Selfish boy, you will come to no good,"* was that your statement at that time?

HENRIETTA ISCARIOT: He was only eight!

EL-FAYOUMY: Eight—and too late!!! Nothing further, great sir!

JUDGE LITTLEFIELD: Cross?

EL-FAYOUMY: No, thank you.

JUDGE LITTLEFIELD: I wasn't asking you.

CUNNINGHAM: Miss Iscariot, what happened the next day?

HENRIETTA ISCARIOT: Well, he ran away from home that night, and I searched for him all day. Late in the afternoon, I observed the following:

MATTHIAS OF GALILEE, *a sad-looking boy, crosses to* JUDAS, *who is spinning his top, alone.*

MATTHIAS OF GALILEE: Hi.

JUDAS: Hi.

MATTHIAS OF GALILEE: Hi.

JUDAS: . . . My name's Judas. What's yours?

MATTHIAS OF GALILEE: Matthias of Galilee.

MATTHIAS OF GALILEE *sits.*

JUDAS: Hey, I got an idea: Why don't you go home and get your spinning top, and then, when you get back with your spinning top, we can play battle of the spinning tops?

MATTHIAS OF GALILEE: I don't got a spinning top.

JUDAS: Oh.

MATTHIAS OF GALILEE:  I wish I had a spinning top, all my
   friends got one except me.

JUDAS:  Yeah, that's rough. I used to not have one, too.

MATTHIAS OF GALILEE:  All the kids, they call me "sissypants"
   'cuz I don't got no spinning top.

JUDAS:  You should ask your mommy to buy you one.

MATTHIAS OF GALILEE:  I don't got a mommy.

JUDAS:  Ask your daddy then.

MATTHIAS OF GALILEE:  I got a daddy, but he's very stern. He
   don't believe in spinning tops, so I can't never get one.

JUDAS:  Wow.

MATTHIAS OF GALILEE:  You prolly think I'm a sissypants, too.

JUDAS:  No. Hey man—don't cry.

MATTHIAS OF GALILEE:  It's just very hard to get through life
   without a spinning top, you know?

*Beat.*

JUDAS:  You . . . You wanna try mine?

MATTHIAS OF GALILEE:  For real?

JUDAS:  Here.

MATTHIAS *spins the spinning top, and his mood immediately
improves.*

MATTHIAS OF GALILEE:  Wow! Nobody in Galilee's got a spinning
   top like this—this is a wicked cool spinning top, Judas.

JUDAS:  I picked it out myself.

MATTHIAS OF GALILEE:  Boy oh boy, your father must really love
   you to buy you such a most definitely dope spinning top as
   this!

JUDAS:  My father's dead.

MATTHIAS OF GALILEE:  What???!!!

JUDAS: The Romans kilt him.

MATTHIAS OF GALILEE (*in one breath*): Yeah? The Romans, they took all our goats last month and now we don't have no money for nothing, even food, and so my father makes me go to the butcher and ask for bones for my dog but I don't have a dog and the butcher knows I don't have a dog, but he gives me the bones 'cuz he takes pity on me and then I give them to my father and he makes soup for us with the bones and we eat it and it tastes really bad and my grandmoms says my father's pride is wounded 'cuz he can't earn no money 'cuz the Romans took our goats and that's why everything's messed up and I can't have no spinning top or nothing . . . Uh-oh!!

JUDAS: What?

MATTHIAS OF GALILEE: I bettah go home now. I have to be home before six. My father's very stern.

JUDAS: Oh. Okay.

MATTHIAS OF GALILEE: Thank you for letting me play with your spinning top, Judas. Maybe someday my daddy'll get some more goats and then I'll get a spinning top, and then I'll come back and play spinning tops with you, and we can play spinning tops and stuff, 'cuz that was really fun.

HENRIETTA ISCARIOT: The sad boy started to leave, then:

JUDAS: Wait. (*Pause.*) Here.

MATTHIAS OF GALILEE: What?

JUDAS: You can have it.

MATTHIAS OF GALILEE: I can have your spinning top?!

JUDAS: Yeah.

MATTHIAS OF GALILEE: For real?

JUDAS: Yeah.

MATTHIAS OF GALILEE: Wow—ee Zow—ee!!! Dag! Thank you, Judas!

MATTHIAS *kisses* JUDAS *on the cheek, exits.*

HENRIETTA ISCARIOT: When people ask me who my son was, I tell them that story.

CUNNINGHAM: Thank you, Miss Iscariot. The witness is excused.

EL-FAYOUMY: Not so fast! Miss Iscariot, your son was picked up by the Roman Authorities the very next day, on a charge of stealing *a blind man's staff*, correct? A Blind man's staff that he then pawned to Omar the Baker to purchase, it says here: "cotton candy and a royal-blue spinning top," correct?! Correct?! . . . Is that correct, Miss Iscariot?!

HENRIETTA ISCARIOT: I don't know, it was so long ago—

EL-FAYOUMY: *Speak into the microphone!!!!!!!*

HENRIETTA ISCARIOT: There is no microphone.

EL-FAYOUMY: Yes. This is true . . . Uh, Your Honor, we have reason to believe that The Staff Deprived Blind Man in question was later run over by a rabid Judean Camel. Here is the death certificate. No further questions.

*Gavel bangs.*

JUDGE LITTLEFIELD: Next witness!

YUSEF EL-FAYOUMY: Yes! Great, wise Sir: Prosecution calls the incomparable Mother Teresa to the stand!

MOTHER TERESA *hobbles up to the stand with a cane. She's old, but tough. She wears her signature sari, and a cross around her neck. She can hear hardly at all.*

BAILIFF: Name.

MOTHER TERESA: Did you say something?

BAILIFF: Name?

MOTHER TERESA: What?

BAILIFF: Your name, please, ma'am?

MOTHER TERESA: Oh. Jess.

(*She checks her watch.*): Ten forty-five. Okay?
BAILIFF: Uhh . . .

EL-FAYOUMY *takes charge.*

EL-FAYOUMY: Mother Teresa: Hello. Over here!
MOTHER TERESA: Who's dat?
EL-FAYOUMY: Hello. It is I, Mother. Remember me?
MOTHER TERESA: Oh, jess. Handsome Boy! Hello.
EL-FAYOUMY: Yes. Hello. How are you?
MOTHER TERESA: Speak louder, boy.
EL-FAYOUMY (*much louder*): I said, "How are you?"
MOTHER TERESA: What?
EL-FAYOUMY (*very, very loud*): *I SAID, "HOW . . . ARE . . . YOU?"*
CUNNINGHAM: Uh, Judge, Bailiff—I believe we do have a hearing device for Mother Teresa?
JUDGE LITTLEFIELD (*to* BAILIFF): Get the device.
BAILIFF: I believe you have the device, sir.
JUDGE LITTLEFIELD: What?! Here.

BAILIFF *takes a large set of earphones, hands them to* MOTHER TERESA.

BAILIFF: Ma'am, put these on, ma'am?
MOTHER TERESA: What?

BAILIFF *puts the earphones on* MOTHER TERESA'*s head.*

MOTHER TERESA: Oh. Thank you, giant man.
EL-FAYOUMY: Yes. Hello Mother! Yes. Can you hear me now?
MOTHER TERESA: Jess.
EL-FAYOUMY (*much softer*): How about now?
MOTHER TERESA: Jess.

EL-FAYOUMY *now simply mimes speaking.*

EL-FAYOUMY: How about that?
MOTHER TERESA: . . . You are tricking me, no?
EL-FAYOUMY: Yes! Yes! I was tricking!
MOTHER TERESA (*playfully*): Bad boy.
EL-FAYOUMY (*playing back*): Very bad! A scandal! Yes! I know.

EL-FAYOUMY *and* MOTHER TERESA *titter.*

CUNNINGHAM: Your Honor, if Prosecution is through flirting
with the beatified iconic virgin, we could, perhaps, begin?
JUDGE LITTLEFIELD: El-Fayoumy, contact has been
established—let's get on with it now, shall we?
EL-FAYOUMY: Without further hesitation, your grace. Forgive the
delay, I was simply enamored to be in her beatific presence,
your eminence. I love Mother Teresa, great one. In Christian
Egypt, she is a great star—as a young boy, I used to don a
towel and my mother's nightgown and stalk the back streets
of Cairo looking for dying things to comfort and salve. Yes.

EL-FAYOUMY *has become a little emotional.*

(*To* MOTHER TERESA): Mother! I love you, really. You are the
Oasis! You are the Light!
JUDGE LITTLEFIELD: Do we need to take a moment here,
counselor?
EL-FAYOUMY (*dabbing his eyes*): Yes. Yes, Your Honor. Perhaps
we do.
JUDGE LITTLEFIELD: Five minute recess! Adjourned.

*Gavel bangs.*

*Lights cross-fade to* SAINT PETER *and* SAINT MATTHEW *sitting in a
quiet place up above.*

SAINT PETER: My name is Peter. They got a Basilica named after me in Rome, which is ironic, 'cuz, back in the day, if you even said the word "Rome" in my presence—more than likely I'd a beat you with my stick. I even had a standing rule on my fishing boat that was strictly enforced: "Talk about Rome, and your ass can swim home alone." I had to have those kinda rules laid down strong 'cuz my younger brother Drew and his friends—they liked to waste their time talkin' about overthrowing Rome and the coming of the Messiah instead a focusing on the task at hand—and I'd always be like: "Look fellas, unless your Messiah gonna come down right now and help us catch some *fish*, then, y'all need to shut the heck up and put your undivided focus on these damn *nets*." Then, one day, Drew didn't turn up for work, then he come runnin' up to me at the shore at the end of the day when I'm bringin' the boat back in talkin' 'bout: "This is Jesus, bro—he's the Messiah. I ain't fishin' no more. I'm just gonna follow him" . . . And this Jesus, who resembled a Messiah about as much as I resemble a ballerina in a tutu, strides on up to me and says: "Catch any fish today?" And I says: "No I did not catch any fish today," and he says: "Take the boat back out to the Sea and you gonna catch some fish." So, I took Jesus out with me—intending to throw his ass overboard—but then he says: "Cast your nets wide and deep," so I did, and then . . . well . . . All I can say is, I'm a damn professional commercial fisherman. No one knew the Sea and its tides better than me. There weren't no fish out there . . . but . . . that's because it turned out they was all in my net. And then Jesus said: "Follow me and I will make you a fisher of men." And what I didn't know then was that I would never see the Sea again.

SAINT MATTHEW: My name is Matthew. I was a Jewish tax collector for the Empire. My job was to take the food out of your mouth and see it shipped off to Rome. Roman tax was exorbitant and non-negotiable. If you had six geese, I took three. If you had a flock of sheep, I took fifty percent. If you had only one sheep, I cut that sheep in half. If you had no sheep, I took a child—your child—and had him or her sold into slavery to settle your debt to the Emperor. This is not a made-up story. This is history. This is fact. We were a conquered nation and I was a traitor to my people. I was a Jew stealing from Jews. According to our laws, I was a sinner and a traitor, I was unclean—unfit to be gazed upon. That's who I was.

SAINT PETER: I hated your ass to look at it.

SAINT MATTHEW: And I looked at you, Peter, as a dumb, ignorant fisherman.

SAINT PETER: And I looked at you, Matthew, as something I can't say in mixed company.

SAINT MATTHEW: I was a scumbag.

SAINT PETER: True 'Dat.

SAINT MATTHEW: I was a scumbag, and it was against the law to look me in the eye. Jesus, he looked me in my eye. That's all he did. He looked me in my eye and he said: "Follow me." And before I knew it, I had. And before we broke bread that night, I was clean again . . . (*Beat.*) I was *clean*.

*Lights fade as the gavel bangs.*

JUDGE LITTLEFIELD: El-Fayoumy, are we ready to proceed?

EL-FAYOUMY *rises.*

EL-FAYOUMY: Absolutely! . . . Forgive me the delay . . . Mother Teresa—I will not take much of your time here, and, certainly, you are in no need of introduction.

MOTHER TERESA: I don't mind.

EL-FAYOUMY: Very well, then . . . Mother Teresa, you are a soon-to-be-canonized saint and a recipient of the Nobel Prize for Peace. You are from Albania, which tells me you know how to handle a firearm, but yet, from the age of twelve, you desired to serve God, at eighteen you entered the convent, and at twenty-one, you left for the slums of Calcutta, and soon after began ministering to the sick and dying—which you did with mercy, love, grace, and generosity for the rest of your life until the day you died. Correct?

MOTHER TERESA: Jess.

EL-FAYOUMY: Yes. Absolutely yes, Mother. Now then, Mother, I call you to the stand today for a special purpose.

MOTHER TERESA: And what is dat?

EL-FAYOUMY: Yes. I am coming to it . . . Mother, your life and subsequent canonization suggest to me that you know a thing or two about God and the life of the spirit—correct?

MOTHER TERESA: I know what I know. What do you want to know?

EL-FAYOUMY: Yes. Mother. Is there a Hell?

MOTHER TERESA: I hope not, but I think so.

EL-FAYOUMY: Judas Iscariot—he is in Hell—yes?

MOTHER TERESA: Well, we can't never know for sure, but it doan look good.

EL-FAYOUMY: Mother, shouldn't we feel sorry for someone in Hell?

MOTHER TERESA: Very sorry. Jess.

EL-FAYOUMY: Does God feel sorry for people in Hell?

MOTHER TERESA: More sorry than us. Jess.

EL-FAYOUMY: But, if God feels so sorry, why not bring the "damned" upstairs? "Three hots and a cot," yes? Surely God has that power?

MOTHER TERESA: Boy, God can lead us anywhere, but sometimes, the people, they doan wanna go. And if the people doan wanna go, then, whaddya gonna do?

EL-FAYOUMY: But surely, these people do not prefer to go to Hell?

MOTHER TERESA: You'd be surprised. Do you know what despair is, boy?

EL-FAYOUMY: Mother, illuminate me.

MOTHER TERESA: I will tell you what Thomas Merton—who was a very handsome boy like you—I will tell you what dat boy had to say about despair. You may not know this, but I at one time in my life suffered a great spiritual darkness—

EL-FAYOUMY: Oh no, not you—

MOTHER TERESA: Quiet now, boy. Jess, for many, many years, I experienced a terrible pain of loss, of God not wanting me, of God not being God, and of God not really existing. One day, I confided my feelings to a friend: an Irish Nun, one of the Sisters of Loretto from Dublin, Ireland. My friend, Sister Glenna, she quoted to me Thomas Merton on the subject of despair. She said:

SISTER GLENNA *appears.*

SISTER GLENNA: "Despair . . . is the ultimate development of a pride so great and so stiff-necked that it selects the absolute misery of damnation rather than accept happiness from the hands of God and thereby acknowledge that He is above us and that we are not capable of fulfilling our destiny by ourselves."

MOTHER TERESA: Do you understand what I'm saying to you?

EL-FAYOUMY: Can you repeat it?

MOTHER TERESA: Jess, sure:

SISTER GLENNA: "Despair . . . is the ultimate development of a pride so great and so stiff-necked that it selects the absolute misery of damnation rather than accept happiness from the hands of God and thereby acknowledge that He is above us and that we are not capable of fulfilling our destiny by ourselves."

EL-FAYOUMY: Ah, yes. I think I see.


SISTER GLENNA *vanishes.*


MOTHER TERESA: Judas, he succumb to despair. The music of God's love and Grace kept playing, but he, he made himself hard of hearing—like me, no? I need this earphone device to hear you, jess? Without them, I can no hear nothing. Judas, he threw his earphones away—and dat is very sad, but dat is what he chose and dat is what happened.

EL-FAYOUMY: But Mother, couldn't God have just obtained a megaphone and simply shouted instructions into Judas's ear?

MOTHER TERESA: Boy, one must participate in one's own salvation. In order to hear, one must be willing to listen. When you turn off God, you are saying: "I know better than you." No good, boy. No good.

EL-FAYOUMY: No good indeed. Mother, you are a ravishing delight and I thank you for your astute and expert testimony!

JUDGE LITTLEFIELD: Cross?

CUNNINGHAM: Mother Teresa, upon receiving your Nobel Prize, did you say to the world, quote: "The biggest obstacle to Global Peace in the world today is abortion"?

MOTHER TERESA: Jess. I said dat.

CUNNINGHAM: Do you actually believe that?

MOTHER TERESA: Jess, I do.

CUNNINGHAM: You accepted large cash donations from the Duvalier family in Haiti, correct?

MOTHER TERESA: Jess.

CUNNINGHAM: Duvalier being a dictator who murdered and stole from his people?

MOTHER TERESA: He gave. I took.

CUNNINGHAM: Blood money?

MOTHER TERESA: No. Cashier's check.

CUNNINGHAM: You also took money from Charles Keating, the savings-and-loan scam artist who robbed American citizens of billions of dollars?

MOTHER TERESA: For the poor, I took it. You got five dollars? I take from you, too.

CUNNINGHAM: You opposed the Vatican II reforms, which among other things, called for a long-overdue official condemnation of anti-Semitism as it relates to the death of Christ. Did you oppose Vatican II, Mother Teresa?

MOTHER TERESA: Jess.

CUNNINGHAM: You blamed the wars of the world on abortion, took blood money from murderers and thieves, and opposed taking a stance against anti-Semitism. I'm having trouble understanding why we're supposed to consider you an expert on anything having to do with the spirit.

MOTHER TERESA: Oh, jess?

CUNNINGHAM: Yes.

MOTHER TERESA: Then maybe you better figure it out.

CUNNINGHAM: I had two abortions, Mother Teresa, what do you think about that?

MOTHER TERESA: I will pray for you and your children.

CUNNINGHAM: I don't have any children.

MOTHER TERESA: Not anymore, and dat's terrible.

CUNNINGHAM: Mother Teresa, if abortion is so terrible, then how come I'm not in Hell?

MOTHER TERESA: I don't know. Did anybody tell you you weren't?

CUNNINGHAM: Must be nice to have all the answers.

MOTHER TERESA: Must be hard to have only questions.

CUNNINGHAM: I can live with my questions, Mother Teresa. But if you can live with those answers, then, with all due respect, I'd say your place is not in Heaven with the Saints, but with the rest of the dinosaurs living in the Stone Age. Nothing further.

EL-FAYOUMY *rises emphatically.*

EL-FAYOUMY: Mother Teresa—I wonder if you join me in wondering just (*turning to* CUNNINGHAM) *who the hell defense counsel thinks she's speaking like that to??!!*

MOTHER TERESA: It's okay, boy. Everybody wanna say something—

EL-FAYOUMY: —Yes—

MOTHER TERESA: —Nobody wanna listen nothing.

EL-FAYOUMY: This is correct, Mother. And on that well-struck note, Mother, let us now go back and address some of the outlandish—

MOTHER TERESA *rises.*

MOTHER TERESA: I go now.

EL-FAYOUMY: But I'm not finished.

MOTHER TERESA: I go now.

EL-FAYOUMY: Oh . . . As you wish, Mother.
(*To jury*): And I think we should all emblazon in our memories—

MOTHER TERESA *takes off her earphones.*

MOTHER TERESA: Boy.

EL-FAYOUMY: Yes, Mother?

MOTHER TERESA: Maybe, Boy, you give this earphone device to Girl. Like this, maybe Girl gonna hear something make her head don't hurt no more.

CUNNINGHAM: There's nothing wrong with my head!

JUDGE LITTLEFIELD: Cunningham, stand down!

MOTHER TERESA: Nice boy . . . Handsome boy . . .

*And time stands still as we see* MOTHER TERESA *hobble off with* BAILIFF.

*Gavel bangs.*

CUNNINGHAM: Defense calls Simon the Zealot to the stand.

SIMON *enters, carrying a staff.*

JUDGE LITTLEFIELD: Name.

SIMON THE ZEALOT: Simon the Zealot.

CUNNINGHAM: You were one of the twelve apostles, Simon—correct?

SIMON THE ZEALOT: Yeah.

CUNNINGHAM: And you were a zealot.

SIMON THE ZEALOT: Yeah.

CUNNINGHAM: Was Judas Iscariot a zealot?

SIMON THE ZEALOT: Well, he didn't go to the meetings or nuthin', but, yeah, he was pretty much a zealot if you ax me.

CUNNINGHAM: Zealots being Jews seeking an end to the violent oppression of the Roman occupation, correct?

SIMON THE ZEALOT: Actually, not exactly, no.

CUNNINGHAM: Are you saying the zealots were *in favor* of the occupation?

SIMON THE ZEALOT: Nah. Not at all. We hated the Romans—absolutely we wanted their pagan asses to hit the curb runnin' and bloody, but we was also opposed to any gentiles in Palestine—Greek, Roman, whoever. What us zealots was really about was promoting a strict adherence to the Mosaic Law.

CUNNINGHAM: Mosaic Law being?

SIMON THE ZEALOT: The Law of Moses—the Torah. That was the whole bag right there, miss. Get rid of the bad seeds and unite the people under the Holy Law of God. Basically, we were the street version of Caiaphas the Elder except we had knives and shit and we thought Caiaphas was soft.

CUNNINGHAM: Soft how?

SIMON THE ZEALOT: With the Romans. He was a bit of a politician, ya know?

CUNNINGHAM: And what was life like under Roman rule?

SIMON THE ZEALOT: Where you from, miss?

CUNNINGHAM: New York.

SIMON THE ZEALOT: Okay: Imagine New York was taken over by, like, Violent Devil-Worshipping Cannibals who spit on your laws, stole all your money, took your women and children as slaves, and put giant swastikas on all your bridges, tunnels, libraries, and civic institutions . . . and anybody that complained about it got nailed naked to a piece of wood in Times Square—left to be eaten by rats, and shit on by pigeons until the weight of their body asphyxiated them to death. That's what it was like.

CUNNINGHAM: And you thought Jesus was going to change that, didn't you?

SIMON THE ZEALOT: We all did.

CUNNINGHAM: Change it how?

SIMON THE ZEALOT: Throw them out. That's what the Messiah was supposed to do.

CUNNINGHAM: But he didn't do that, did he?

SIMON THE ZEALOT: Nah.

CUNNINGHAM: And yet he was capable of it, wasn't he? You saw him perform miracles, raise people from the dead.

SIMON THE ZEALOT: It was a bit of a conundrum, yeah.

CUNNINGHAM: Were you at the disturbance at the Temple?

SIMON THE ZEALOT: Yeah.

CUNNINGHAM: What did you think about that?

SIMON THE ZEALOT: Ya kiddin'? I loved it. Judas, too. We all did. We thought it was on, ya know?

CUNNINGHAM: "On" meaning?

SIMON THE ZEALOT: The beginnin' of the revolution.

CUNNINGHAM: But it wasn't, was it?

SIMON THE ZEALOT: Nah.

CUNNINGHAM: What happened after the riot at the Temple?

SIMON THE ZEALOT: Jesus had us all retreat to this house, then, he was like: "I'm going to die soon, so let's just chill."

CUNNINGHAM: Must have been very disappointing.

SIMON THE ZEALOT: It was confusing—I mean, whacked-out shit, man. One minute Jesus is beating infidels down—and I'm talking fists and whips—Jesus was whipping ass, knockin' out teeth, screaming he's gonna tear down the Temple, the next minute, he's all passive. And we were all like: We invested three years in this guy, and now he's gonna just lay down? It didn't seem to make no sense.

CUNNINGHAM: Simon: Why do you think Judas Iscariot turned Jesus in to the authorities?

SIMON THE ZEALOT: Personally, I think Judas was trying to throw Jesus into the deep end of the pool—make him swim.

CUNNINGHAM: Judas was testing Jesus?

SIMON THE ZEALOT: Not testing, 'cuz we all knew Jesus had mad skills pass the test.

CUNNINGHAM: What then?

SIMON THE ZEALOT: Lissen, I knew Judas pretty good. We was pretty tight on account of, ya know, our politics and whatnot. What I believe is this: Judas knew that if the Romans grabbed up Jesus, that Jesus would have to act.

CUNNINGHAM: Meaning?

SIMON THE ZEALOT: Meaning *Act*. Get it on and start kicking ass like He was supposed to. Emancipation was our birthright. That's what the Messiah was there for. I think, personally, that Judas did what he did to help Jesus realize his destiny and fulfill his mission.

CUNNINGHAM: Judas tried to help Jesus?

SIMON THE ZEALOT: I believe so. Yes.

CUNNINGHAM: Thank you.

EL-FAYOUMY *rises.*

EL-FAYOUMY: So . . . Judas was a "helper," eh?

SIMON THE ZEALOT: Yeah.

EL-FAYOUMY: Just . . . there to lend zee helping hand, yes?

SIMON THE ZEALOT: Yeah.

EL-FAYOUMY: Yes. Yes, I think you are correct, Zealous one! Because, for me, I know that if *my* best friend were to sell me out and betray me for a roll of quarters, causing me to be beaten, whipped, gouged, and mangled, and then strung up and left to be baked by the Hot Judean Sun till I resembled a shriveled-up, bearded *frankfurter*—Why Yes!

I'm sure my first thought as I gasped for air and bled to death would be, "Really, that Judas—what a *helpful* guy!—Oh, yes, I must remember to send him zee Thank-You *note*"!! . . . . . . Simon the Zealot, let's talk turkey: Judas was your friend, yes?

SIMON THE ZEALOT: Yeah.

EL-FAYOUMY: You thought the same way, yes?

SIMON THE ZEALOT: Yeah.

EL-FAYOUMY: Shared the same opinions.

SIMON THE ZEALOT: Yeah.

EL-FAYOUMY: Had the same beliefs.

SIMON THE ZEALOT: Yeah.

EL-FAYOUMY: Wanted the same things.

SIMON THE ZEALOT: Yeah.

EL-FAYOUMY: Wanted them desperately.

SIMON THE ZEALOT: Yeah.

EL-FAYOUMY: Then why, Zealot, did you not do like Judas did? If you believed what you believed and thought what you thought, why, Zealot, did you not join Judas or turn Jesus in on your own? Can you explain me this?

SIMON THE ZEALOT: . . . I don't know.

EL-FAYOUMY: Protecting a friend—that is admirable indeed. Zealot, Jesus never said his mission as Messiah on Earth was to overthrow the Romans, did he?

SIMON THE ZEALOT: Not exactly, no.

EL-FAYOUMY: You wanted it to be the mission, you even thought it was the mission, but it wasn't really the mission, was it?

SIMON THE ZEALOT: I guess not.

EL-FAYOUMY: How is it, Zealous One, that *you* came to understand that violence wasn't part of Jesus's mission, but *Judas* never did?

SIMON THE ZEALOT: . . . I couldn't say.

EL-FAYOUMY: Answer me this: What was your inner life like before you met Jesus of Nazareth? And I don't think I need to advise you to be honest here, do I?

SIMON THE ZEALOT: Nah. I was consumed with anger. Jesus— he saved my life.

EL-FAYOUMY: Man of Zeal: Final Question: Do you believe, as the Bible says, that God made man in his own image?

SIMON THE ZEALOT: I do.

EL-FAYOUMY: Of course you do, and there, Zealous friend, lies the answer to one of my previous questions. The difference, I posit, between you and Judas Iscariot is that you *accepted* that you were created in God's Image, whereas Judas Iscariot—he sought to create God into *his own image*—God as earthly avenger, which was not God's way. And even though you were scared, Zealot, even though you were confused and angry, and hurt, still, you chose to obey God, didn't you?

SIMON THE ZEALOT: I guess I got lucky.

EL-FAYOUMY: Luck indeed! Simon the Zealot: There is something beautiful about you—and that—is your modesty. You are a God-Fearing Man. Go now. Be free.

CUNNINGHAM *rises.*

CUNNINGHAM: Jesus never proclaimed himself to be God, Simon—correct?

SIMON THE ZEALOT: Nah. He never did.

CUNNINGHAM: What did Jesus say to Judas at the last supper?

SIMON THE ZEALOT: He said, "Do what you gotta do."

CUNNINGHAM: Sounds like Jesus approved.

SIMON THE ZEALOT: Maybe.

CUNNINGHAM: But if you were Judas, Simon, and "doing what you had to do" ended up getting you thrown into despair and hanging from a tree and then sent to Hell to live in misery and infamy in perpetuity—if you were Judas— wouldn't you have kinda wished that Jesus had maybe said something else instead?

SIMON THE ZEALOT: Yeah, counselor. I very much would have.

CUNNINGHAM: Would it kind of make you feel like you got fucked?

EL-FAYOUMY: Objection: Language! "A foul mouth is a dirty bird"!

CUNNINGHAM: I withdraw the question.

SIMON THE ZEALOT: . . . I woulda felt like you said, though.

CUNNINGHAM: Thank you, Simon. Nothing further.

SIMON *exits.*

JUDGE LITTLEFIELD:  Next witness!

EL-FAYOUMY:  Most reverent señor—with your magisterial permission—Prosecution now conjures Satan—Prince of Darkness, to the stand!

SATAN *enters, waves amiably to the jury.*

JUDGE LITTLEFIELD:  Name!

SATAN (*to* CUNNINGHAM):  Fabiana Aziza Cunningham, right?

JUDGE LITTLEFIELD:  Lou.

SATAN:  I been keeping the light on for ya, Cunningham.

JUDGE LITTLEFIELD:  C'mon now, Lou—why don't you take your seat and we can get started here?

SATAN:  You never change, Frank, do you?

JUDGE LITTLEFIELD:  I suppose I don't.

SATAN:  I like that about you. Now say, how's Wilhemina doing? And the girls?

JUDGE LITTLEFIELD:  I wouldn't know. Now, park your caboose in that chassis if you would, please?

SATAN:  I'm sorry. Of course.

(*To* EL-FAYOUMY):  Fire away.

(*To* JUDGE):  My apologies, Frank.

BAILIFF *enters.*

JUDGE LITTLEFIELD:  Bailiff!

BAILIFF:  I was helping the elderly, sir!

JUDGE LITTLEFIELD:  Let's just proceed. El-Fayoumy—proceed!

EL-FAYOUMY:  Ah. Yes. Uh . . . Yes . . . Uh . . . How are you today, Satan?

SATAN:  Well . . . Long night, but uh, no regrets.

EL-FAYOUMY:  Up late partying with the decadent and debauched?

SATAN:  Oh, God, does it show?

EL-FAYOUMY: Oh—No no, not at all.

SATAN: I'll tell ya—I could barely make it through my double-session Pilates this morning—if it weren't for the good genes, I'd be a raisin with tits and a perm.

EL-FAYOUMY: Yes. Well, you look very good. Sincerely. Really, Satan, you have an excellent physique.

SATAN: Oh—Thank you. So do you.

EL-FAYOUMY: Oh. Thank you, too. Yes, I make exercises . . . Anyway, so . . . No horns and tail today, Prince of Evil?

SATAN: No.

EL-FAYOUMY: At the dry cleaners, I suppose.

SATAN: Yes.

EL-FAYOUMY: Yes . . . . . . . . I must say, Claimer of the Damned, your candor is quite refreshing.

SATAN: As is yours.

EL-FAYOUMY: Oh . . . Thank you . . . Yes . . . Oh! Your jacket, Satan, really, it is smart.

SATAN: You like it?

EL-FAYOUMY: Beautiful, really. Armani?

SATAN: Gucci.

EL-FAYOUMY: "Gucci." Yes. Elegant. Very. Yes . . . So . . . (And your trousers, they are Gucci, too?)

SATAN: Yeah.

EL-FAYOUMY: They have a lovely sheen . . . Anyway, let's begin then, shall we?

SATAN: I am at your service.

EL-FAYOUMY: I appreciate that.

SATAN: And I appreciate your appreciation.

EL-FAYOUMY: Excellent . . . So . . . Dark One, tell me: Did you ever have any conversations with Judas Iscariot prior to his selling-out of Jesus Christ?

SATAN: No, I did not.

EL-FAYOUMY: Sure about that?

SATAN: Quite sure, yes.

EL-FAYOUMY: Never "entered into him," as I believe Saint
Luke's Gospel puts it?

SATAN: No.

EL-FAYOUMY: And again, you are more or less sure of that?

SATAN: Ask my main squeeze, Sheila: If I had "entered" Judas
Iscariot, trust me, he woulda felt my considerable
"presence"—if you know what I mean.

EL-FAYOUMY: Yes—you and Jimmy Woods—I've heard the
rumors. So then, it would be safe to say that the "Devil
didn't make him do it"?

SATAN: Absolutely—Unless, of course, there's some other
Devil runnin' around that I don't know about.

EL-FAYOUMY: Very funny. Really, you are quite charming,
Satan . . . But let us be quite clear: You did nothing,
Satan, nothing, to sway Judas Iscariot towards
selling out Jesus of Nazareth, Prince of Peace? Correct?

SATAN: Correct.

EL-FAYOUMY: Not even a tiny nudge?

SATAN: Honestly, he didn't require nudging. Judas was a
gimme—It happens like that sometimes.

EL-FAYOUMY: A "gimme," yes. A bad seed.

SATAN: Yes.

EL-FAYOUMY: Yes. Well, then, how 'bout after he did the deadly
deed? Did you speak with the Savior Betrayer then?

SATAN: I spoke to him, yeah.

EL-FAYOUMY: Care to share?

SATAN: Not a problem. I appeared to Mister Iscariot at
Bathsheba's Bar and Grill shortly after the night in question.
I was actually in town for a guy named Abdul Mazzi-Hatten,
but he never showed. When I encountered Mister Iscariot,
he appeared to have already taken full advantage of the
Happy Hour.

JUDAS *crosses to playing area. He is very drunk and very troubled.*
SATAN *meets him.*


Oh. Hello, friend. How are you this evening?

JUDAS: "How am I this evening?"—what are you, a fuckin'
maître d', man?

SATAN: I'm Clementine. Clementine of Cappadocia.

JUDAS: Yeah?! Well, why don't you go home and fuck your
mother, Cappa-douche-a, okay?!

SATAN: "Doe-sha"—Cappa-doe-sha.

JUDAS: What??!!

SATAN: It's Cappa-doe-sha.

JUDAS: Well, lemme ask you something—Cappa-douche-ah—
Do I look like someone who gives a flying fuck right now
about where the fuck you're from?!

SATAN: I'm very sorry.

JUDAS: Sorry don't mean shit, dick! Take all the "sorries" in
the world, pile 'em one on top of the other, ya know what
you got, Cappa-douche? You got a big pile a fuckin' nuthin'
is what you got! Okay?

SATAN: You're right.

JUDAS: You wanna do somethin' about it??!!

SATAN: No, sir.

JUDAS: Then go fuck your mother and leave me the fuck alone!

SATAN: I will. Thanks for the advice.

JUDAS: Hey!!! . . . Where you going?!

SATAN: It seems like you preferred to be alone.

JUDAS: Why would I prefer that?! What're you saying: I look
like some kinda Lone Wolf? Like a fuckin' piranha, bro?

SATAN: Do you mean Pariah?

JUDAS: I mean what I mean. Whaddya—need a light or
something?

SATAN: Oh. Thanks.

JUDAS: Like this lighter?

SATAN: Very nice.

JUDAS: I bought it today, man. Expensive shit, but—I got it like that.

SATAN: I can see you're a man of wealth and substance. I admire that.

JUDAS: "Wealth and substance"—don't push it. So, what's your name?

SATAN: . . . Clementine. Clementine of Cappadocia.

JUDAS: Clementine, eh? Isn't that a girl's name?

SATAN: Not in Cappadocia.

JUDAS: Well, it is here, bro—you sure you ain't a girl, man?

SATAN: Pretty sure, yeah.

JUDAS: I'm Judas, Judas Iscariot—maybe you heard of me?

SATAN: Nah, man—I'm from out of town.

JUDAS: You never heard of me?

SATAN: Nope.

JUDAS: You don't get around much, do ya, Clementine? So whereabouts you from, man—Egypt?

SATAN: Cappadocia.

JUDAS: That's in Egypt, though, right?

SATAN: No—Cappadocia is in Cappadocia.

JUDAS: I dig your pyramids, man—and the sphinx?
(to BARTENDER): Bartender! Hey! More of that Mesopotamian Wine for my Nubian friend! And some dates and figs, too!
(To SATAN): You smoke opium, Clam?

SATAN: Clem.

JUDAS: And some opium, bartender—the good stuff!

SATAN: You seem like a man on a mission.

JUDAS: Took this girl to a puppet show today, man.

SATAN: Yeah? How was it?

JUDAS: Fuckin' sucked. Puppets are bullshit, ya know?

SATAN: In Cappadocia, we burn puppets!

JUDAS: Well, you people got the right idea over there—That Pharaoh, he's a smart man. Yeah, man. Hey, Clammy—Cheers!

SATAN: Cheers!

JUDAS: Yeah.—Whoa! Hey man, thass a nice shirt, what you pay for it?

SATAN: Two pieces of silver.

JUDAS: Two pieces of silver? HA!!!! I'll give you five. Here ya go, switch shirts with me.

SATAN: But, I'm rather fond of this shirt.

JUDAS: C'mon, man—switch shirts—switch shirts. We're buds now, friends an' shit—I'll let you be my wingman—get you laid, bro!

SATAN: A nice brunette?

JUDAS: Two brunettes and a eunuch! C'mon, strip!

SATAN: Oh, okay.

*They switch shirts.*

(*To audience*): He was so drunk, he didn't even notice my unmistakably Satanic stench.

JUDAS: Yo, I dig this shirt, what is it? Silk?

SATAN: From Cappadocia.

JUDAS: Fuckin' Cappadocian Silk!! All right!

SATAN: Your shirt is nice, too.

JUDAS: Yeah?

SATAN: Yeah.

JUDAS: Wow . . . . . . . . . . Thanks, man. That's a nice thing to say. Yeah. Been a while since I heard something nice. That's really nice, bro.

*Beat.*

Hey, man, if I told you something corny, would you think that I was, like, a dick?

SATAN: Not at all.

JUDAS: Okay . . . I'm kinda mildly afraid of going to Hell.

SATAN: Why?

JUDAS: Minor incident last night—a miscalculation on my part—nothing serious.

SATAN: Well, one thing I can tell you about Hell: As an eternal destination, it's apparently vastly underrated.

JUDAS: Yeah?

SATAN: And "Hell" is nothing more than the Absence of God, which, if you're looking for a good time, is not at all a bad thing. You wanna play the lute, sing Mary Chapin Carpenter—that's what Heaven's for. You wanna rock? Apparently, Hell's the venue.

JUDAS: Are there, like, girls down there?

SATAN: Not many, but I hear they import them from developing nations on weekends . . . But hey, I wouldn't worry about going to Hell.

JUDAS: Even if I did something, perhaps, a little controversial?

SATAN: God understands.

JUDAS: Yeah, but, don't choices have, like, consequences?

SATAN: C'mon, you really think we have a choice?

JUDAS: Well, don't we?

SATAN: Okay: Did you pass by that fuckin' disgusting, stinky, fuckin' leper on your way in here tonight?

JUDAS: Who? Freddy?

SATAN: "Freddy," yeah: You think *he* had a choice, Freddy, stinkin it up out there, can't scratch his balls for fear a pullin' out his testes? Huh? And what about what's-his-face from the old days—Job? Don't you think if Job had a choice he woulda been like: "Okay, God, enough! I get the fucking point"?!

JUDAS: Yeah, but, Job did say that!

SATAN: Yes he did! And what happened next, Judas? God kept right on fucking with him until Job made the only choice available—which was to quietly keep his wrinkly ass-cheeks spread wider than the Red Sea till God got tired of drilling him for oil!

JUDAS: I guess . . . But say . . . Ah, never mind.

SATAN: What?

JUDAS: Not important.

SATAN: C'mon.

JUDAS: Okay. Well, say, what if someone were to betray, for example . . . the Messiah—

SATAN: —You mean the *Messiah,* messiah?

JUDAS: Yeah. Say some idiot had a choice to betray the Messiah or not betray him, and he chose to betray him?

SATAN: Gee, I couldn't say. Whadda you think?

JUDAS: I'd say the guy's fucked, right?

SATAN: I really couldn't say.

JUDAS: C'mon Clams, I'm just askin'.

SATAN: Well, since you asked, I guess I'd say that if this guy—

JUDAS: 'Cuz this is just some hypo-theoretical guy here—

SATAN: Right. I'd say that if this clown we're talking about betrayed the Messiah, that, probably, *"it would've been better for that man if he had never been born."*

JUDAS: Never been born???!!!

SATAN: Hey—you asked.

JUDAS: That's heavy, man. That's a fuckin' heavy trip, man, Clams.

SATAN: I'm thirsty—how 'bout you?

JUDAS: That's fuckin' really heavy.

SATAN: Let's have another round here, Pops! Two barrels of wine and a hooker menu!

(*To* JUDAS): You okay, man?

JUDAS: Clams, man, I haven't been laid in three years, bro. Can ya believe that—guy like me?

SATAN: Three years?

JUDAS: I wasted my prime, man. And then I wasted my prime after my prime.

SATAN: Well, I think you'll prolly get fucked tonight, bro.

JUDAS: Ya think so?

SATAN: Yeah. I'm pretty sure.

JUDAS: I wanna nother fuckin' drink. Tonight man, I'm gonna drink this fuckin' bar!

SATAN: Hey. Judas, lemme ask you something: Who is this Jesus of Nazareth guy I've been hearing about?

JUDAS: Jesus of Nazareth?

SATAN: Yeah—I heard he's some kinda somebody.

JUDAS: Some kinda somebody?

SATAN: Yeah, that's what I heard.

JUDAS: Aw, fuck that guy, man—he's a bitch!

YUSEF EL-FAYOUMY *rises triumphantly.*

EL-FAYOUMY: *"FUCK THAT GUY, HE'S A BITCH"!!!!! Your Honor! Nothing further!*

JUDGE LITTLEFIELD: Cross?

CUNNINGHAM: . . . Not at this time.

JUDGE LITTLEFIELD: Lou, stick around.

SATAN: I know the drill.

*The gavel bangs.*

JUDGE LITTLEFIELD: Meal break! Fifteen minutes!

EL-FAYOUMY: Fabiana, free for lunch?

*Gavel bangs. Lights fade.*

*Cross-fade to* JUDAS's *lair.* JESUS *is there with his bucket, alone.*

# "SIC DEUS DILEXIT MUNDUM"

SAINT MONICA *appears with* MARY MAGDALENE.

SAINT MONICA: Hey, y'all. This is Mary Mags—she the only bitch I let hang with me up here. Tell 'em whatchu gotta say.

MARY MAGDALENE: My name is Mary of Magdala. I was a disciple of Jesus, I was present at the crucifixion, and I was the first person He appeared to after the resurrection.

SAINT MONICA: Bitch got *clout!*

MARY MAGDALENE: I was one of the founders of the Christian faith, and I was known for my ability, in times of difficulty, to be able to turn the hearts of the Apostles towards the Good.

SAINT MONICA: The good!

MARY MAGDALENE: Some people think I was a whore.

SAINT MONICA: Misogynist bitches!

MARY MAGDALENE: Other people think Jesus was my husband.

SAINT MONICA: Femin-o-tic bitches!

MARY MAGDALENE: I was not a whore.

SAINT MONICA: "Pimps up, Hos *Down!*"

MARY MAGDALENE: I was an unmarried woman in a town of ill repute.

SAINT MONICA: *Ill* repute!

MARY MAGDALENE: And also, I was not the wife of Jesus either.

SAINT MONICA: Still love ya!

MARY MAGDALENE: But, I am pretty sure that I was his best friend. We shared an intimacy that I cannot put to words except to say we saw into each other's hearts and were in love with what we found . . .

SAINT MONICA: Love!

MARY MAGDALENE: I also knew Judas Iscariot very well.

SAINT MONICA: Gangsta!

MARY MAGDALENE: Out of the Twelve, he was the most moody and the most impetuous, and yet, he was my favorite.

SAINT MONICA: Tupac!

MARY MAGDALENE: And in some ways, I think he was Jesus's favorite too . . . Judas was almost an alter ego to Jesus—he was the shadow to Jesus's light. He was the sour to the sweet and the cool to the warm. They often walked together, more often than not arguing—no one could get a rise out of Jesus like Judas could. I can remember times when Jesus emerged from an argument with Judas positively furious—shaking his head wildly, snorting, and clicking his teeth, red-faced with exasperation—and he would tell me what they had been fighting about—still agitated—but, inevitably, he would end up staring into space and sighing—smiling. I think that if someone were to say that Judas was good for Jesus that they would not be mistaken . . .

SAINT MONICA: Not mistaken!

MARY MAGDALENE: When I think of Judas, my heart breaks.

SAINT MONICA: But Mary Mags: If we are all eternal, and if Human Life is only the first mile in a *billion,* do you honestly believe that God could abandon any mothahfuckah so soon in the journey?

MARY MAGDALENE: I don't know. Jesus never talks about it. That's how I know His heart hurts worse than mine.

*The gavel bangs.*

JUDGE LITTLEFIELD: Next witness!

CUNNINGHAM: Defense calls Sigmund Freud, Your Honor.

BAILIFF: Name!

SIGMUND FREUD: Doctor Sigmund Shlomo Freud.

CUNNINGHAM: Doctor Freud, would it be accurate to say you qualify as an expert in the field of modern psychiatry?

SIGMUND FREUD: Fräulein—I AM modern psychiatry.

EL-FAYOUMY: Objection, Your Honor!—the witness is boasting!

JUDGE LITTLEFIELD: Overruled!

EL-FAYOUMY: But a "boaster," Your Eminence—it is distasteful, really!

JUDGE LITTLEFIELD: Siddown, El-Fayoumy!

EL-FAYOUMY: I lunge to obey you, your grace—but let the record reflect that Prosecution has grave reservations about this man's alleged so-called "standing" as a psychiatric expert!

SIGMUND FREUD: Perhaps a quick jaunt to London for a leisurely perusal of "The Standard Edition of *The Complete Psychological Works of Sigmund Freud Volumes One Through Twenty-Four*" would set your mind at ease.

EL-FAYOUMY: *Perhaps it would if you were indeed* . . . . . . . . . . . Oh. I see. Right. Yes. Of course. Uh . . . Yes.

*He sits.*

CUNNINGHAM: Doctor Freud, you are, in fact, the "Founder of Psychoanalysis," correct?

SIGMUND FREUD: I am.

CUNNINGHAM: You maintained a private practice in neuropathology for nearly a half century; is that not so?

SIGMUND FREUD: It is.

CUNNINGHAM: You were on the cover of *Time* magazine in an issue dedicated to the greatest scientific minds of the twentieth century.

SIGMUND FREUD: I was.

CUNNINGHAM: Are you familiar with the case history of one Judas Iscariot?

SIGMUND FREUD: Most certainly.

CUNNINGHAM: Doctor Freud, in your expert opinion, can a suicide victim be precertified as psychotic?

SIGMUND FREUD: Without question. Man's instinct for self-preservation is his most supple and reflexive muscle. When that muscle fails, it is because his mind has failed. A decision to take one's own life can only be precipitated by a failure of the mind—an irrational rebellion against man's most basic instinct—to endure and live. Therefore, yes—the victim of suicide must be precertified as, indeed, psychotic.

CUNNINGHAM: In your expert opinion, Doctor Freud, was Judas Iscariot a psychotic?

SIGMUND FREUD: Without question.

CUNNINGHAM: And are psychotics responsible for their actions?

SIGMUND FREUD: No, they are not. For example, say I have a bad bout of influenza. As a result of my bad influenza, I sneeze rudely, but involuntarily, in your face. The next day, you wake up with the same flu. Did I cause your flu? No. My flu caused your flu. I only sneezed because I was sick.

CUNNINGHAM: In your opinion, Doctor Freud, does Judas Iscariot belong in Hell?

SIGMUND FREUD: No, he does not.

CUNNINGHAM: Explain.

SIGMUND FREUD: Suicide is a direct sign of mental illness.

CUNNINGHAM: But did he become mentally ill *after* allegedly betraying Jesus of Nazareth, or was he mentally ill to begin with?

SIGMUND FREUD: Preprogrammed, yes. You must understand: Normal people do not kill themselves—even under extreme duress.

CUNNINGHAM: And what would you say to people who would

say that Judas brought about his own mental illness by betraying Jesus and getting him crucified?

SIGMUND FREUD: I would say this: Number One, you cannot conjure or "bring about" mental illness. Number Two, any God who punishes the mentally ill is not worth worshipping. And, Number Three: "an ounce of prevention is worth a pound of cure"—the person who could have prevented this tragedy was Jesus, not Judas. He chose not to.

CUNNINGHAM: But isn't Judas responsible because he did what he did of his own free will?

SIGMUND FREUD: Fräulein, I once had a suicidal patient leap through my fourth-floor window to her death. She exercised her free will—did I bill her estate for the broken plate-glass window she leapt through? Of course not! My friend Winston Churchill, who provided me safe haven from the Nazis in 1938, likes to say: "The price of greatness is *responsibility*." I believe firmly in taking responsibility. So, after the unfortunate woman's death, I exercised responsibility for *my* greatness—by moving my offices to the ground floor. I should think God would have done the same.

CUNNINGHAM: Your witness.

EL-FAYOUMY: Doctor Freud, yes, sorry for the mix-up before.

FREUD *yawns big and disdainfully.*

SIGMUND FREUD (*re: the yawn*): Excuse me.

EL-FAYOUMY: So, Herr Doktor—I must admit I am intimidated to be in the midst of such greatness. After all, you are a "genius," correct?

SIGMUND FREUD: Correct.

EL-FAYOUMY: An "expert"?

SIGMUND FREUD: Yes.

EL-FAYOUMY: A big brain.

SIGMUND FREUD: Unequivocally.

EL-FAYOUMY: Yes. "Unequivocally." Yes. Nice word. And it rolls off your tongue so effortlessly—really, I am impressed.

FREUD *again yawns big and disdainfully.*

A little tired, are we, Doctor? Perhaps a kilo or two of *fine-grade Bolivian flake* would restore your pep?!

SIGMUND FREUD: Excuse me?

EL-FAYOUMY: Cocaine, Doctor! "Blow," "Flake," "Rock"— "She don't lie"—does she, Doc?!!!

SIGMUND FREUD: What?

EL-FAYOUMY: Over a twelve-year span, you consumed cocaine in what can only be categorized as Prodigiously Massive Quantities, correct?

SIGMUND FREUD: As part of my research, yes.

EL-FAYOUMY: "Research"—yes. And after twelve years of round-the-clock research, you finally came to the conclusion that ingesting staggering amounts of powder up your nose was, perhaps, unhealthy?

SIGMUND FREUD: I was trying to determine its medicinal value.

EL-FAYOUMY: Is that your real nose?

SIGMUND FREUD: Your mother denied you her breast, didn't she?

EL-FAYOUMY: I'll thank you to let me ask the questions, Doctor Fried.

SIGMUND FREUD: *Freud!*

EL-FAYOUMY: Oh, yes, Freud, of course. Forgive me, I made a "you"-slip, didn't I? . . . Anyway, last question Mr. Expert Genius: Doctor Freud: You were an avowed atheist all your life, correct?

SIGMUND FREUD: Correct.

EL-FAYOUMY: And then you died and found out what?

SIGMUND FREUD: I experienced anti-Semitism as a child—it prejudiced me against all religion.

EL-FAYOUMY: Einstein experienced prejudice—but he wasn't wrong like you, was he? My cousin Wagui can't count to ten without drooling, but he wasn't wrong like you either, was he? Was he??!!

SIGMUND FREUD: Intelligence and Faith are two different things!

EL-FAYOUMY: Are they, Doctor Freud? Because I would say that you can't have one without the other. But, of course, I'm not a brilliant genius expert like you, am I?

SIGMUND FREUD: I had a wonderful vibrant mind and my intellectual curiosity was boundless!

EL-FAYOUMY *makes a violin-playing gesture.*

EL-FAYOUMY: Good day, doctor, go blow your nose—you are excused!

CUNNINGHAM (*rising*): Doctor Freud, do sane people commit suicide—yes or no?

SIGMUND FREUD: No!

(*Towards* EL-FAYOUMY): Though they can sometimes be tempted to *murder!*

EL-FAYOUMY: Go murder an eight-ball, egghead!

JUDGE LITTLEFIELD: That's enough! Next witness!

*Gavel bangs.*

Next witness!

EL-FAYOUMY: Irresistibly Alluring Majesty. Prosecution calls Legendary Hawaiian Singer and Popular Entertainer Don Ho to the stand!

JUDGE LITTLEFIELD: Don Ho's not dead!

EL-FAYOUMY: Oh . . . Well, thank god for that. In that case, Prosecution calls Caiaphas the Elder, High Priest of the Sanhedrin, to the stand!

JUDGE LITTLEFIELD (*rising*): Right . . . Ladies and gentlemen of the jury, at this time, I must excuse myself from these proceedings until such time as said witness has concluded testimony. Before his ascension into the Lap of the Lord, Caiaphas the Elder and I were partners in a successful chain of Kosher Pizza Parlors in East Purgatory—For that reason, at this time, I must step down. *Bailiff!!!* Get your ass over there, put on those glasses, and adjudicate—pronto! Proceed.

JUDGE *exits as* EL-FAYOUMY *approaches* CUNNINGHAM.

EL-FAYOUMY: Fabiana, may I borrow a pen?

CUNNINGHAM: Only if I can shove it through your eye.

EL-FAYOUMY (*confidentially*): Fabiana, how can I prove my sincerity to you? Even though you are always here and I am always here—still—I think of you when you aren't here even though you are always here.

BAILIFF: Next witness, please!

EL-FAYOUMY: Yes—I obey.

(*To* CUNNINGHAM): Later we shall discuss.

(*To* BAILIFF): Yes. Julius zee Bailiff, correct? May I call you Julius?

BAILIFF: All right.

EL-FAYOUMY: How about Jules?

BAILIFF: I guess.

EL-FAYOUMY: So tell me J—shall we commence?

BAILIFF: That'd be good.

EL-FAYOUMY: Wise J: Prosecution calls Caiaphas the Elder!

CAIAPHAS *enters.*

Caiaphas the Elder, High Priest of the Sanhedrin, hello to you.

CAIAPHAS THE ELDER: Hello.

EL-FAYOUMY: "Shalom"—as it were.

CAIAPHAS THE ELDER: Shalom.

EL-FAYOUMY: Caiaphas the Elder: Perhaps you can clear this up—is there a Caiaphas the Younger?

CAIAPHAS THE ELDER: No.

EL-FAYOUMY: And yet, you are the Elder?

CAIAPHAS THE ELDER: Yes.

EL-FAYOUMY: I see. Yes. Thank you. My cousin Amghad Wahba owes me five bucks now. So, Caiaphas the Elder: In the Bible, it says that Judas Iscariot made an approach to you—a dark and nefarious approach—to offer up the location of Jesus of Nazareth, and to, in fact, turn him in to you and the authorities. Correct?

CAIAPHAS THE ELDER: Correct.

EL-FAYOUMY: Caiaphas the Elder: Are you saying that it was Judas Iscariot who approached you, and not the other way around?

CAIAPHAS THE ELDER: Yes.

EL-FAYOUMY: Because I saw in a film once, Caiaphas the Elder, where it was *you* who approached *him*.

CAIAPHAS THE ELDER: It was Judas Iscariot who approached me at the Temple, not the other way around.

EL-FAYOUMY: Yes. But still, even though your statement is indeed confirmed by all four Gospels, Caiaphas the Elder, I must ask you again: Did you approach Judas Iscariot about betraying his leader and Messiah, Jesus of Nazareth?

CAIAPHAS THE ELDER: I did not.

EL-FAYOUMY: Why not? Jesus was a big headache to you, no? You were legitimately concerned that the high jinks of Jesus would lead to an uprising and a resulting crushing Roman Massacre of your Jewish people in retribution, weren't you?

CAIAPHAS THE ELDER: I was.

EL-FAYOUMY: So, why not reach out and touch someone, Caiaphas the Elder?

CAIAPHAS THE ELDER: Are you asking me why I didn't try to approach one of the Apostles initially?

EL-FAYOUMY: Yes.

CAIAPHAS THE ELDER: I didn't think it would work.

EL-FAYOUMY: Why not?

CAIAPHAS THE ELDER: There is an old rabbinical saying: "Let them kill you, but do not cross the line." During my eighteen-year reign as head of the Sanhedrin and Guardian of the Temple, I dealt with countless Messiahs, zealots, rebels, and fanatical believers. My experience in these matters taught me: They get killed, yes, but as a rule—they do not cross the line.

EL-FAYOUMY: "Cross the line," yes—this means what?

CAIAPHAS THE ELDER: To betray your ideals. Your conscience. The law.

EL-FAYOUMY: Judas crossed that line, didn't he?

CAIAPHAS THE ELDER: He did.

EL-FAYOUMY: He betrayed the ideal in betraying Jesus—The Rabbinical Ideal. He crossed the line.

CAIAPHAS THE ELDER: Yes.

EL-FAYOUMY: Do you admire that?

CAIAPHAS THE ELDER: No. I do not.

EL-FAYOUMY: But why not? We all cross the line sometimes, don't we?

CAIAPHAS THE ELDER: We are all capable of crossing the line. Thankfully, we do not all do it.

EL-FAYOUMY: But really, Caiaphas the Elder, what's the big deal? You cross a line, so what? Just draw yourself another line, correct?

CAIAPHAS THE ELDER: No. Not correct.

EL-FAYOUMY: Why not?

CAIAPHAS THE ELDER: The line comes from God, doesn't it? The line is given. We do not create it, and thus, it is not ours to modify. It is only ours to Obey or Betray.

EL-FAYOUMY: I see. Caiaphas the Elder: When *Pontius Pilate* first arrived in Judea, he visited you in the Temple, did he not?

CAIAPHAS THE ELDER: He did.

EL-FAYOUMY: And as a show of his force and might, Pontius Pilate attempted to place symbols of Rome in the Temple, which was, to your people, a great desecration of your Holy place of worship, correct?

CAIAPHAS THE ELDER: Correct.

EL-FAYOUMY: It would have constituted a worshipping of False Idols, yes?

CAIAPHAS THE ELDER: Yes.

EL-FAYOUMY: Caiaphas the Elder, when you saw Pontius Pilate attempting this, what did you do?

CAIAPHAS THE ELDER: I told him that he must remove the pagan symbols.

EL-FAYOUMY: And what did Pilate say to that?

CAIAPHAS THE ELDER: I believe the gist of his reply was: "What are you gonna do about it, Curly?"

EL-FAYOUMY: And what *did* you do?

CAIAPHAS THE ELDER: . . . I knelt before him—

EL-FAYOUMY: —and begged for mercy?

CAIAPHAS THE ELDER: No.

EL-FAYOUMY: Groveled for forgiveness?

CAIAPHAS THE ELDER: No! I removed my headdress, bared my throat to him, and bade him slit it.

EL-FAYOUMY: In other words, Caiaphas the Elder, you "let him kill you, but you did not cross the line."

CAIAPHAS THE ELDER: I guess so. Yes.

EL-FAYOUMY: You did not cross the line!

CAIAPHAS THE ELDER: No. I did not.

EL-FAYOUMY: Judas crossed it, though—didn't he?

CAIAPHAS THE ELDER: He did.

EL-FAYOUMY: Interesting. And, by the way, what was the result of your standoff with Pilate regarding the sanctity of the Temple?

CAIAPHAS THE ELDER: Pilate backed off.

EL-FAYOUMY: He didn't put up the pagan symbols, did he?

CAIAPHAS THE ELDER: No.

EL-FAYOUMY: You held the line.

CAIAPHAS THE ELDER: Yes.

EL-FAYOUMY: Your integrity castrated him, didn't it—his little Roman balls rolling down the Temple hill like withered purple grapes! Yes?!

CAIAPHAS THE ELDER: I have no response to that.

EL-FAYOUMY: As well you shouldn't! Now then, last question: Caiaphas the Elder, it has been said that in Western Culture, the most prized virtue is Honesty, but in Eastern Culture— which would include Judea at that time—in Eastern Culture, the most prized virtue was and is Loyalty. Caiaphas the Elder: Do you agree with said hypothesis?

CAIAPHAS THE ELDER: Counselor, there are six hundred thirteen Sacred Laws in our Torah. Complying with these Laws requires Honesty *and* Loyalty. But the most important requirement of The Law is *Obedience* to it. That is what is most prized.

EL-FAYOUMY: Yes. Fair enough. But in your opinion, was Judas Iscariot "loyal"?

CAIAPHAS THE ELDER: Obviously not.

EL-FAYOUMY: Was he "honest"?

CAIAPHAS THE ELDER: No.

EL-FAYOUMY: Caiaphas the Elder: Was Judas Iscariot obedient?

CAIAPHAS THE ELDER: To his own will and desires—yes. I believe that he was.

EL-FAYOUMY: And to service that will and those desires, Judas crossed the line. Didn't he?

CAIAPHAS THE ELDER: He served a necessary purpose, but as a fellow Jew, I confess he disgusted me.

EL-FAYOUMY: Caiaphas the Elder, I thank you—and may I add, you are much more handsome in person than when they portray you on the silver screen!

CUNNINGHAM *rises*.

CUNNINGHAM: "High Priest of the Sanhedrin"—that was an extremely powerful and prestigious position in Judea—correct?

CAIAPHAS THE ELDER: Correct.

CUNNINGHAM: In fact, except for the Roman governor and King Herod, the "High Priest" was, in actuality, the most powerful position *in* Judea, was it not?

CAIAPHAS THE ELDER: Yes.

CUNNINGHAM: Would you mind looking me in the eye when you respond to a question?

CAIAPHAS THE ELDER: My position was very important. As High Priest, I maintained the Sacred Laws, the safety of the populace, and our tradition.

CUNNINGHAM: Caiaphas—Is there a reason you won't meet my gaze? Or is ignoring women simply another component of the tradition you were charged to maintain?

EL-FAYOUMY (*rising*): Objection, Julius! The witness is not just a Holy Man—but a very Holy man! Defense counsel is aware she is a juicy pulchritudinous dish—and yet, the witness is being berated for merely avoiding the salacious temptations of her intoxicatingly firm and fervently aromatic flesh! I move to censure, really!!

CUNNINGHAM: I withdraw the question.

EL-FAYOUMY: Sexy Vixen—you are warned!

BAILIFF: Hey!

EL-FAYOUMY: Oh! Julius! Yes! Forgive me! She makes my organs bounce! Yes. Uh.

(*To* CUNNINGHAM): Sorry.

(*To* BAILIFF): Yes.

*He sits.*

CUNNINGHAM: Caiaphas, you stated to the Prosecution that Judas Iscariot "crossed the line" and that he "disgusted you"—correct?

CAIAPHAS THE ELDER: Correct.

CUNNINGHAM: Well then maybe you can help me out here, because I'm a little confused. Judas Iscariot handed Jesus of Nazareth over to you, correct?

CAIAPHAS THE ELDER: Yes.

CUNNINGHAM: And then *you* handed Jesus of Nazareth over to Pontius Pilate, correct?

CAIAPHAS THE ELDER: I did.

CUNNINGHAM: So what exactly is the difference between you and Judas Iscariot—'cuz unless I'm missing something here, I fail to see it.

CAIAPHAS THE ELDER: Between me and Judas? Big difference.

CUNNINGHAM: Caiaphas, you were a rabbi and a Jew. Jesus was a rabbi and a Jew. Is it not crossing the line for one rabbi to hand over another rabbi to be killed by pagans?

CAIAPHAS THE ELDER: Jesus was a blaspheming, seditious rabbi, and I did not know for sure that he would be killed.

CUNNINGHAM: But the penalty for sedition was crucifixion, correct?

CAIAPHAS THE ELDER: That was the Roman charge, not mine.

CUNNINGHAM: Yes. Your charge was Blasphemy—and what was the penalty for Blasphemy, Caiaphas?

CAIAPHAS THE ELDER: Your Honor, I will not sit here and be blamed for the death of Christ yet again!

CUNNINGHAM: No one's blaming you for the death of Christ, Caiaphas. I'm simply asking you a question which I am directing you to answer now before this court: You charged Jesus with Blasphemy. What was the penalty for Blasphemy, Caiaphas?

CAIAPHAS THE ELDER: "Stoning, followed by hanging."

CUNNINGHAM: So then, how can you sit there and pretend that you didn't know for sure that Jesus of Nazareth would be killed?

CAIAPHAS THE ELDER: Jesus could have easily saved himself.

CUNNINGHAM: Saved himself how?

CAIAPHAS THE ELDER: By retracting his Blasphemous claims! Our Torah has six hundred thirteen Sacred Laws—I can't even count how many Jesus broke or treated with wanton disregard and disdain! He broke the laws that came from the God of Abraham, Isaac, and Jacob! He violated the word of God. He violated the Laws of Moses. He consorted with the Unclean, and women, and prostitutes. He performed Miracles on the Sabbath, He proclaimed himself Messiah! He forgave sin! *Who was he to forgive sin?!* Only God can do that! If that's not crossing the line, then I don't know what is!!

CUNNINGHAM: Jesus was fulfilling your Old Testament prophecies of Isaiah to the letter—

CAIAPHAS THE ELDER: —He was also fulfilling the prophecies in Deuteronomy which warned against "False Messiahs and Marvel workers"! It would have been one thing had he confined himself to the forests and rivers spouting his ravings as the Baptist did, but at the Great Temple?! I would have been derelict not to put a stop to it. He was whipping people! Kicking them. Threatening to destroy the Temple! Calling it a Den of Thieves! If someone did that in your Saint Patrick's Cathedral, would you not arrest them?!

CUNNINGHAM: And yet, Judas Iscariot, who came forward in the face of this "great threat," is in your eyes not a patriot, but a traitor. A traitor who, in your words, "disgusted you." Why is that, Caiaphas?

CAIAPHAS THE ELDER: Because he handed Jesus over for money.

CUNNINGHAM: And why did you hand Jesus over, Caiaphas?

CAIAPHAS THE ELDER: The words and deeds of Jesus were leading towards rebellion—and the price of rebellion under Roman rule was a bloodbath. A massacre, Counselor. So I determined that it were better to have one man dead than a thousand—that's why.

CUNNINGHAM: I see. So, you were looking out for the Common Jewish Man, is that correct?

CAIAPHAS THE ELDER: I was.

CUNNINGHAM: Were you a Common Jewish Man, Caiaphas?

CAIAPHAS THE ELDER: In the eyes of God, we are all the same.

CUNNINGHAM: But how about in the eyes of the Common Jewish Man? You were seen as an Aristocrat, weren't you?

CAIAPHAS THE ELDER: I came from wealth.

CUNNINGHAM: Would you say that you were popular with the Common Jewish Man?

CAIAPHAS THE ELDER: My job was a sacred one—not a popularity contest.

CUNNINGHAM: The high Temple taxes that you inflicted on your people, would you say that made you more popular with the Common Jewish Man or less popular?

EL-FAYOUMY: Objection, Your Honor! Vixen is badgering!

BAILIFF: Sustained!

CUNNINGHAM: The exchange rates at the Temple were also extremely unfavorable to the Common Jewish Man, and the purification pools outside the Temple—where the Common Jewish Man was required *by law* to be cleansed before being permitted to enter the Temple—the purification pools were not free either, were they?!

BAILIFF: Cunningham!

CAIAPHAS THE ELDER: No no, I'll answer: The laws were the laws and the rates were the rates.

CUNNINGHAM: And did you have a sliding scale for the poor?

CAIAPHAS THE ELDER: No.

CUNNINGHAM: So the poor—who constituted a large percentage of the Common Jewish Man at that time—remained impure and unclean and were denied the right of worship.

CAIAPHAS THE ELDER: You've made your point.

CUNNINGHAM: No, I don't think I have! Your position, Caiaphas, did not require you to be popular with the Common Jewish Man, did it?!

CAIAPHAS THE ELDER: My position required me to answer to God.

CUNNINGHAM: Did God appoint you High Priest of the Sanhedrin?

CAIAPHAS THE ELDER: It was with God's Blessing—

CUNNINGHAM: —It was with *Rome's* blessing, Caiaphas! You were appointed by *Rome,* and at the end of the day, for the eighteen years you served, that's who you had to answer to, and that's who you were required to be popular with! And the day you showed Rome that you couldn't handle your own people was the day you'd have been thrown out on your ass—isn't that true?!

CAIAPHAS THE ELDER: I belonged to God, not Rome! My job was to uphold the six hundred thirteen Sacred Laws, and to protect my Temple and my People—and that's what I did!

CUNNINGHAM: And was not Jesus of Nazareth one of your people, Caiaphas?! Whether he was a messiah, or a prophet, or a Holy Man, or a crazy man—was he not one of your own?! And was it not considered the height of treachery to betray Jewish blood to your oppressors?! Come on, Caiaphas! Tell us that it did not prick your conscience to turn Jesus, a fellow Jew, over to the Romans! Tell us that handing over a fellow rabbi to his certain death at the hands of the enemy didn't violate your sense of "crossing the line" and your knowledge of the law! Tell us, Caiaphas, that at the end of the day, there was a *difference*—in the eyes of *God*—between what you did and what Judas did!

*Beat.*

This is Purgatory, Caiaphas—I've got all day.

CAIAPHAS THE ELDER: . . . In terms of result: No difference.

CUNNINGHAM: How about in terms of follow-through: Judas recanted and tried to return the silver, did he not?

CAIAPHAS THE ELDER: He did.

CUNNINGHAM: And did you, Caiaphas, do anything at all to try to prevent Jesus's death?

CAIAPHAS THE ELDER: No.

CUNNINGHAM: And therein lies the real difference between you and Judas Iscariot, does it not? And yet, you sit here and say how Judas "crossed the line" and that he "disgusted" you! And if that's true, Caiaphas, then I wonder, how you must've felt about yourself.

CAIAPHAS THE ELDER: That's between me and God.

CUNNINGHAM: Well then for your sake, Caiaphas, I sure hope that your God has a more forward-thinking attitude than Judas's God does. Step down, you're excused.

EL-FAYOUMY: Caiaphas the Elder, Judas approached you—correct?

CAIAPHAS THE ELDER: Yes.

EL-FAYOUMY: He didn't have to approach you, Caiaphas the Elder, did he?

CAIAPHAS THE ELDER: No.

EL-FAYOUMY: And yet he did.

CAIAPHAS THE ELDER: Yes.

EL-FAYOUMY: Of his own free will.

CAIAPHAS THE ELDER: Yes.

EL-FAYOUMY: And accepted payment for his betrayal.

CAIAPHAS THE ELDER: Yes.

EL-FAYOUMY: Payment. Judas did not say, "Caiaphas the Elder, put your money away, mister, this one's on the arm," right?

CAIAPHAS THE ELDER: Right.

EL-FAYOUMY: Caiaphas the Elder, I think we all realize the precarious position you were in, trying to protect your citizens from Roman reprisal.

CAIAPHAS THE ELDER: And it makes you feel good to say that, doesn't it? After two thousand years of persecution and vilification, you finally get around to saying: "Hey, we know it wasn't you and your people's fault." Is that it?

EL-FAYOUMY: Good Caiaphas the Elder, I was only trying to—

CAIAPHAS THE ELDER: Win your case, right? I tell you what: You people call me, I come. You question, I answer—but please—never say that you realize the position I was in, because you have no idea the position I was in. And never try to excuse or forgive me, because I'm not interested in your forgiveness. God's forgiveness: This interests me. Yours? I could care less. Why? Because you have no idea. The people who need forgiving? The people who perpetrated the lies and exaggerations that became sacrosanct fact and led to hatred and violence for the past two thousand years? They are the ones who need forgiving—and not by you—but by me—me—and my people. It's the Writers of the Gospel who need forgiveness—not me. No, sir. I know what it is to suffer. Do you? I don't think so.

(*To* BAILIFF): Julius: My best to Frank.

EL-FAYOUMY: You're very handsome, Caiaphas.

CAIAPHAS THE ELDER: If I am, it's 'cuz God made me, not 'cuz you said so. Good day.

CAIAPHAS *ambles off wearily. Gavel bangs. Cross-fade to* SAINT THOMAS.

SAINT THOMAS: My name is Thomas. At the Last Supper, I was the first one to say that I would die for Jesus, and I was also the first one to head for the hills doing ninety when the Romans came and arrested him. And then, when Jesus resurrected himself, I was also the guy who said I wouldn't believe He was who He said He was unless I could see with my own eyes the holes in His hands and personally inspect them and touch them—as if I was some qualified medical examiner, like Quincy or something. But the thing of it was, Jesus showed them to me. And not only that, He let me touch them. In a ministry based entirely on the virtues of Faith, He gave me proof. I had no Faith, and he gave it to me for free. I don't know why I got the benefit of my doubt, and Judas didn't get help with his. And I'm not saying this 'cuz I liked the guy—'cuz personally, I thought Judas was a bit of a jerk-off. Actually, "fuckin' dick" would be more accurate. Judas was the kinda guy—at least with me—where, one minute he's your friend, and the next minute, he's

making fun of you in front of everybody. He used to like to
say that the reason Jesus had to do the Miracle of the Loaves
and the Fishes was because I ate all the food when no one
was looking. Stuff like that. But then other times, he could
be real nice, like, once we were partnered together to go
into town to heal people and cast out demons, and well, I
had some problems that day—everyone I tried to heal ended
up getting worse. In fact, this one lady I almost blinded and
another guy started going into convulsions—but Judas fixed
it. He healed them—he really did—and that tells me his faith
was genuine. And when we got back to camp that night, he
didn't tell anybody how I messed up. In fact, he said I did a
good job, and I appreciated that. I knew Jesus knew it was
bullshit, but I appreciated the gesture. I thought it showed
largeness on Judas's part. And the thing is, Judas was kind of
a dick, but he wasn't shallow or petty. He really was pretty
large. He wasn't the best, but he was far from the worst.
Jesus liked him, liked him a lot, in fact. Judas was right up
there in the top three with Mary Magdalene and Peter, who,
by the way, could also be a dick sometimes, too. The trick
with Peter was: Never talk about fish. The guy was crazy for
fish. Say something wrong about a fish and forgettaboutit.
The guy would go crazy. Anyways—some people say Judas
did what he did 'cuz he was greedy. Personally, I think that's
bullshit. The guy wasn't wandering around the desert for
three years with Jesus and a bunch of ragamuffins like us
'cuz he was looking to get rich. Other people say that The
Devil got into him. Again, bullshit. Judas was loyal to a fault.
Obsessively loyal, even. Judas would have taken on The
Devil and his entire army, one against a thousand, if he had
to, and he woulda done it with relish. Other people say
Judas did it 'cuz he knew the ship was sinking and he was
trying to get himself a nut to have something to fall back on.

Lissen: Judas was not a "fall-back" guy, he was one hundred percent "fall forward." And to me, that deserves some consideration. I was not fall forward. Not by a long shot. And neither were most of the others. Judas was a dick, but he deserved better. Just one Saint's opinion.

JUDGE *enters.*

Next witness!

CUNNINGHAM: . . . Your Honor, at this time, Defense would like to introduce exhibit A-fourteen, *ancient surveillance footage* of an event that occurred less than twenty-four hours after Jesus's arrest. Lights, please.

*A squad room in Jerusalem.*

SOLDIER 1: Pilate gonna kick yo ass!

SOLDIER 2: Pilate gonna see that ass—he gonna kick it two times!

SOLDIER 3: Yo—when Pilate see this mothahfuckah's ass, he gonna be like: "Centurion! It's time to whup ass!"

SOLDIER 1: He gonna rape yo wives!

SOLDIER 2: He gonna take yo cattle!

SOLDIER 3: He gonna kick yo cattle's ass, too!

SOLDIER 1: And yo sheep and yo lambs!

SOLDIER 2: Pilate gonna cancel yo granmutha's WIC check, B!

PILATE *enters.*

PILATE: What's all this damn ruckus about?!

SOLDIERS: All hail Pontius Pilate: Hail, hail, hail!

PILATE: Is there a problem here?

SOLDIER 1: Judas is trying to recant!

PILATE: Hold up a minute, who?!

SOLDIER 3: Judas Iscariot—from the Jesus of Nazareth crew.

SOLDIER 2: This stinky mothahfuckah right here!

JUDAS: Jesus is an innocent man—please, please—

SOLDIER 1: Should we start whupping ass now?

JUDAS: He's innocent! Please. Please. Jesus is innocent.

PILATE: C'mon now, Judas, them "San-who-saids"—hold up a sec.

(*To* SOLDIER 2): Yo Curt—what they call themselves?

SOLDIER 2: Sanhedrin, sir.

PILATE: Right. Judas, them SandHeadsSons paid you thirty pieces of silver, now that's four months' wages, that ain't no chicken feed.

JUDAS: I made a mistake, please, please, you don't understand, man—

PILATE: I understand perfectly. You sold out your brother, now you feel guilty, so you tryin' ta come in here talkin' 'bout "It was dark, I kissed the wrong muthahfuckah," but we Romans, man—Romans don't dance that song.

JUDAS: I'm recanting—

PILATE: You can't recant!

(*To his boys*): Hey, fellas, remember the last Semite strolled up in here talkin' 'bout "I recant"?!

(*To* JUDAS): Believe me, J-Crew, you doan wanna do that. Whatchu need to do is relax, brother—take the wifey to a puppet show, sumpthin'. This ain't nuthin' but a little PR opportunity before the holidays, thass all—

JUDAS: —But he's innocent. Please. Please—

PILATE: Hey now, lissen: Judas, we don't give no good goddamn 'bout this Jesus—He just a muthahfuckah talks a lotta shit. Everybody talks shit, even *I've* been known to talk a little shit on the once in a while. Thing is: We ain't tryin' to lay down no heavy charge on that Nazareth boy—

we just gonna beat down his ass a little, make them
Sanhen-ja-call-its happy so's we can all live in peace. I mean:
Dontchu wanna live in peace, Judas? Ain't that what it's all
about?

I mean after all, brother, ain't like we lookin' to crucify
the muthahfuckah!

*Fade back to courtroom.*

CUNNINGHAM: Defense calls Pontius Pilate!

EL-FAYOUMY: *I object!*

JUDGE LITTLEFIELD: On what grounds?

EL-FAYOUMY: On the grounds that it is objectionable!

JUDGE LITTLEFIELD: Overruled!

EL-FAYOUMY: But, your holiness, really, it *is* objectionable: I
sense it, although I cannot put it into words.

JUDGE LITTLEFIELD: Overruled!

BAILIFF: Name!

PILATE: Pontius Pilate.

CUNNINGHAM: Pontius Pilate?

PILATE: That's right, baby.

EL-FAYOUMY (*rising*): But are you a *licensed* pilot?!

JUDGE LITTLEFIELD: Siddown, El-Fayoumy!

CUNNINGHAM: Pontias Pilate . . . Judas Iscariot came down to
your tent to recant his testimony—correct?

PILATE: On the advice of counsel, I cite my right to plead the
Fifth Amendment.

CUNNINGHAM: You then told Judas Iscariot that Jesus was only
gonna receive a "beat down," correct?

PILATE: On the advice of counsel, I cite my right to plead the
Fifth Amendment.

CUNNINGHAM: You bear responsibility for the death of Jesus

Christ—not Judas Iscariot, but you— Isn't that correct, Pontius Pilate?!

PILATE: On the advice of counsel, blah blah blah.

(*To* JUDGE): Your Honor, I got a two p.m. tee time—can I go now?

JUDGE LITTLEFIELD: This won't take long, Pontius.

CUNNINGHAM: Judas came to your office and begged you on bended knee to take the money and release Jesus, and you refused him! Judas recanted. He tried to return the money— first to the Sanhedrin and then to you. Do you deny that?

PILATE: Hey, if I had messed up as bad as that cat had, I woulda tried to rebate them ducats, too.

CUNNINGHAM: So you admit that Judas did try?

PILATE: No. I do not admit that he tried. Did you hear me admit that?

CUNNINGHAM: We all know what happened, Pilate—We just saw the tape!

PILATE: Ain't nuthin' on that "so-called" tape implicates me of anything but trying to find a peacefully nonlethal solution to a potentially incendiary problem.

CUNNINGHAM: Right. Mister Pilate, you were the Fifth Prefect of Judea, correct?

PILATE: Correct.

CUNNINGHAM: A "Prefect" being what?

PILATE: Governor. Also known as "Procurator." My official title was "Hedg-e-mon."

CUNNINGHAM: "Hedg-e-mon"?

PILATE: Translated from the Greek, it means "Excellency."

CUNNINGHAM: I see. And you governed or procurated over Judea from twenty-six to thirty-six A.D., correct?

PILATE: Longest ten years of my life.

CUNNINGHAM: Why do you say that?

PILATE: You ever *been* to Judea, missy? It ain't Paris, France—
believe that.

CUNNINGHAM: I see.

PILATE: Yeah, that Moses musta read the map backwards—
misplaced his bifocals, sumpthin'—'cuz if that was the
"promised land," shit, them Jews shoulda held out for a
better Promise.

CUNNINGHAM: You didn't care for Judea much?

PILATE: Care for it? Armpit of the Empire, if you ask me. No
atmosphere, nuthin'. Hot. Dirty. Dusty. Flies everywhere.
Complete lack of Culture and Amusements. I'd a rather
spent ten years up inside the crack a my ass . . . But Augustus
ordered me to keep the peace there, so I obeyed my
Emperor, and did my duty.

CUNNINGHAM: And kept the peace?

PILATE: The Pax Romana, baby, the prime directive—dass
right.

CUNNINGHAM: And, under your rule, how was the peace kept
in Judea, Mister Pilate?

PILATE: By any means necessary.

CUNNINGHAM: Violently?

PILATE: Violently or otherwise—they was free to have it any
ways they wanted.

CUNNINGHAM: According to Philo of Alexandria, who wrote
about you in forty-one C.E., your tenure as Governor of
Rome was known for its "constantly repeated executions
without trial, wanton injustices, graft, and ceaseless and
grievous cruelty"—care to comment?

PILATE: No, I do not.

CUNNINGHAM: During your reign as Procurator in Jerusalem,
how many deaths did you order?

PILATE: A lot—don't apologize for it either. Them Jews was
rowdy.

CUNNINGHAM: "Rowdy"?

PILATE: Dass right—rowdy. As in: not docile. As in: a muthahfuckah had to put his foot down.

CUNNINGHAM: And you put it down, didn't you?

PILATE: Damn skippy I did. Orders from Rome—what's a brothah to do?

CUNNINGHAM: During your tenure in Judea, how many Crucifixions would you say you ordered?

PILATE: A lot less than my predecessor—that's for damn sure! That muthahfuckah would crucify a Semite for yellin' "Fire" at a barbecue—man would go buck-wild from *jump!* Me? I reduced Crucifixions in Palestine by seventy percent, and now, that's documented.

CUNNINGHAM: Well, that's lovely, Mister Pilate, but I'll direct you now to answer the question posed to you.

PILATE: Which was what?

CUNNINGHAM: How many Crucifixions did you preside over during your time in Jerusalem?

PILATE: I'd say . . . a few hundred—give or take. So what?

CUNNINGHAM: Over seven hundred Crucifixions while you were on assignment in Judea. Does that sound about right?

PILATE: Sound good to me. Sure.

CUNNINGHAM: And you publicly washed your hands of how many of them, Mister Pilate?

*Pause.*

PILATE: I don't know what you mean by that.

CUNNINGHAM: I mean that, other than Jesus of Nazareth, out of over seven hundred Crucifixions and countless executions, did you ever—in any other instance—publicly wash your hands and attempt to abdicate responsibility for your actions, Mister Pilate?

*Pause.*

PILATE: I don't recall.

CUNNINGHAM: You backpedaled because you knew it was wrong, didn't you?

PILATE: Romans don't have backpedals.

CUNNINGHAM: You knew Jesus was a Holy Man or a fool, but whatever he was, you believed him when he said that his Kingdom wasn't on Earth, didn't you?

PILATE: See, now, I don't recall that conversation.

CUNNINGHAM: You don't "recall" that conversation?! You know what, Mister Pilate, why don't you say that again so I can slap a perjury charge on you! You ordered the death of Christ— you and you alone—and then you pawned it off on Jesus's "reticence" and Judas's "impetuousness" and the "politics" of the Sanhedrin and the "rowdiness" of the Jewish people— is that not the case, Pontias Pilate?! Yes or No?!

PILATE: You can go on squawking if you want to—my conscience is clean. What you need to do is take it up with them Jews.

CUNNINGHAM: Mister Pilate, were the High Priests of Jerusalem authorized to order a death sentence?

PILATE: No they were not.

CUNNINGHAM: Was King Herod authorized to issue a death sentence?

PILATE: No he was not.

CUNNINGHAM: How about the Jewish people themselves— were they free to issue death sentences at their whim and fancy?

PILATE: No.

CUNNINGHAM: One man, Mister Pilate. In all of Judea, one man alone had the authority to put another man to death. Who was that man, Mister Pilate?

PILATE: Am I on trial here? 'Cuz lass time I checked, it was your client, Judas Iscariot, freezing his narrow ass off in the ninth Circle of Hell—not me!

CUNNINGHAM: My client recanted with a remorseful heart and was ignored!

PILATE: Then you need to take that up with them Jews, not me. I mean, this ain't some new theory I'm introducing to ya! It's documented. Ain't no Sherlock Holmes/Nancy Drew Mystery here, lady: Them Jews was cantankerous. Ornery. They worshipped a Jealous, Angry, and Vengeful God—and guess what? Surprise, surprise: They was angry, jealous, and vengeful themselves. I never had a problem in Judea wasn't caused by some rabble-rousing, no-account Jew. Believe me, sister—you need to talk to them, not me.

CUNNINGHAM: It's always the Jews, Mister Pilate, isn't it?

PILATE: Well, it sure as shit was in Judea, missy . . .

- CUNNINGHAM: You wanna know what I really think, Mister Pilate? I think this whole story about you hemming and hawing about what to do with Jesus is just a load of made-up crap written by Jewish Christian Evangelists seeking to broaden the appeal of the Jesus story to the Roman Empire. There is nothing that we know about you, Mister Pilate— absolutely nothing—that suggests for even a second that you would have even a passing hesitation about putting *any* Jew to death—let alone a revolutionary figure like Jesus who was being proclaimed the Messiah, who had entered the city of Jerusalem to crowds of cheering supporters, and who had the very next day incited a riot at the Temple. You hated your assignment, you hated Judea, and Mister Pilate, you hated Jews. Hated them. You hated the Jews because they contested you. You hated them because they fought back. You hated them because they clung to their religious beliefs and were willing to die for them. But most of all, I think,

you hated them because you knew they were stronger than
you. I think that bothered you a great deal. I think, Mister
Pilate, that it made you resentful and vengeful and furious. I
think it made you feel small and inadequate. I think it gave
you skin irritations and nervous tics. I think it kept you up
nights and made you count the days until you could return
to the safe, bourgeois comfort of Rome. That's what I think.
I think you're hiding behind historical inaccuracies and
outright lies, Mister Pilate. I think that you're a liar and a
fraud. I think that when Jesus was put before you, you did
not see a God or a prophet, you did not see a lunatic or an
innocent, you didn't even see a human being. I think,
Mister Pilate, that what you saw before you that morning
was just one more Jew, and you didn't hesitate. Why would
you? . . . . . . . You didn't wash your hands, Pontius Pilate—
History did it for you. Isn't that true?

PILATE *rises.*

PILATE: I think I've had enough here.
CUNNINGHAM: If you were a man, Pilate—you'd own up to the
    truth!
PILATE: The truth?! Whose truth you talkin' about, Red? The
    truth is I was made a saint in the Ethiopian Church! The
    truth is I was named a martyr for the Christian Church in
    three-forty-eight A.D. That's the damn "truth"!
CUNNINGHAM: A Christian martyr?
PILATE: Did I stutter, girlie?
CUNNINGHAM: Well, I guess that's what they mean about
    History being "a lie agreed to."
PILATE: A "lie"?! Whatchu know about what's a lie and what's
    the truth?! Whatchu know about my history?! Alls you got
    to go on is some book written four different ways by four

different Jews wasn't even there in the first place! And whatchu know about my life *after* Palestine? Whatchu know about what I mighta did or didn't do when I got back home to the Motherland? Dass right—you don't know jack—do you? They didn't write down that part of the story, did they? Shit—I'm a tell you something: You and your presumptious nature reminds me more and more of my ex-wife Rhonda every minute—and believe me that ain't no compliment! Yes, I met that Jesus boy—seemed like a fine fellow! He dressed like a hobo and smelled like a goat, but give the boy a shave and a shower, and he woulda been basically all right. And I'll tell you something else: Unlike Judas, that Nazarene boy had character. He didn't come up on me begging and groveling—crying like a bitch. He faced me like a man, like a Roman almost, and that impressed me. I was willing to just have him be clubbed in his head for a coupla hours—redirect his youthful energies—but them Jews—they wasn't havin' none a that! You can say what you want to, think what you want to, but them Jews was fixin' to pitch a fit until that boy was served up for lunch like chicken in the skillet! And they had the numbers on us that weekend—two hundred thousand strong converging on the city for they High Holidays and ready to rumble at the drop! I did what I had to do to preserve the damn peace! Why?! 'Cuz that was my damn job! I did my job! I did my damn job and now you wanna call me a liar?! Question my veracity and my character?! I am a Roman, lady! One hundred percent, 24/7, we never close! Underneath my ball sac is stamped: VERITAS! And that means TRUTH! And that means my honor is defined by my integrity and my integrity is defined by my truth! And I defy you—here and now—to produce one shred of evidence to support your wild and defamatory claims! Shit! You better check the résumé two times before

you start tryin' ta sweep your dirt under a Roman's rug! I
am clean like Dove and Ready for Love, missy! I live in
Heaven! Where you live at, girlfriend?! Shit! I'll tell you
what, though: When you get your head straightened out,
gimme a call some time if you want to—I'll take you down
to the Aqueduct for a Pizza and a Tussle. Show you my
tattoos . . . . . . . Any more questions?

CUNNINGHAM: I think, Mister Pilate, that you've told us all we
need to know.

PILATE: Okay, then, I'm a roll out, now, boo—work on my
short game.

JUDGE LITTLEFIELD: The witness is excused.

PILATE (*strutting off magisterially*): Hail Caesar, baby!

EL-FAYOUMY *rises.*

EL-FAYOUMY: Your Excellency! "Hedg-e-mon"! Just one
question if I may?!

PILATE: What's that?

EL-FAYOUMY: Yes . . . I wonder if you would tell the court—
Hedge—the following: If indeed Judas Iscariot came to your
tent to recant—and I'm not saying he did or didn't—and by
the way, the only Gospel that says *anything* at all about Judas
recanting is Matthew, so it's three against one and the one in
question was not only a Greek, but a drunken Greek and a
card cheat—but anyway—please tell us now if you will
please: Good Sir, Hedge, when Judas came to your tent to
allegedly recant, if in fact he did, which, I am in no way
seeking confirmation of herewith, *HOWEVER,* if, by
chance, the gin-soaked Greek was miraculously correct and
Judas did in fact attempt to recant and return the tarnished
silver, tell us please—*AND THIS IS VERY IMPORTANT*—
Hedge: Did you get the sense or impression that Judas was

recanting out of a genuine *REMORSE* and concern for Jesus, *or* do you think he was seeking to undo the damage out of a neck-saving *fear* of the dire consequences and everlasting repercussions of betraying Our Rightful and most Exalted and Just Lord and Savior, Jesus Christ, the Divine Son of Man? . . .

*Beat.*

PILATE: I am a man—and defense counsel may dispute this—who happens to know something about Remorse—personal and otherwise. In my day, I stared into the eyes of perhaps ten thousand accused men and sat in judgment of them. I spared a few, and executed plenty. I sent people to face the whip, the cell, the gallows, and the cross. And I sent a few home, as well. Remorse is rare, but when you see it, it is unmistakable. Judas Iscariot had no Remorse—His Fear left no room for it. His Fear was one hundred percent Ego-Driven and Self-Serving. One hundred percent panic. Zero percent remorse. If you believe nothing else—believe that.

EL-FAYOUMY: "Hedge"—thank you. Thank you, indeed.

*The gavel bangs.*

JUDGE LITTLEFIELD: Next witness!

CUNNINGHAM *rises.*

CUNNINGHAM: Your Honor, Defense reconjures Satan to the stand.

JUDGE LITTLEFIELD: Lou, you can come in now . . . Bailiff! Go fetch him! Go fetch Satan!

BAILIFF: Alone?

JUDGE LITTLEFIELD: Go!

SATAN *enters, quite perturbed.*

Ah! . . . Have a seat, Lou.

SATAN: I want to file a formal fuckin' complaint, Frank!

JUDGE LITTLEFIELD: Aw, this ain't about the turkey roll in the cafeteria again, now, is it, Lou?

SATAN: No, Frank, this is not about the turkey roll in the cafeteria. What this is about, Frank, is I recognized a couple of your court officers at the vending machines, okay? Ask me how I recognized them, Frank.

JUDGE LITTLEFIELD: Lou—

SATAN: No! Don't you fuckin' "Lou" me—you little fag— God's been fuckin' *stealing souls* again, hasn't he?!

JUDGE LITTLEFIELD: El-Fayoumy! Escort the jury out!

EL-FAYOUMY: Yes. Right this way, please.

SATAN (*to* BUTCH, *as* EL-FAYOUMY *leads them out*): And you! Honeywell! You're on my fuckin' list, hayseed—so don't expect any last-second reprieves. Shorts and tank tops, Stretch—pack light!

*They exit.*

JUDGE LITTLEFIELD: This is unacceptable behavior, Lou.

SATAN: Don't tell me what's unacceptable—Those two court officers were mine, Frank—their souls in Hell, safe and secure! What? I don't got enough to contend with?—*now* I gotta deal with God cruisin' the barnyards of Hell poaching condemned poultry like some kind of silver-fox-tailed thief in the fuckin' night?? This is bullshit, Frank, and you know it—and I'm not leaving here this time without my satisfaction—so you better do something about it right fucking now!

JUDGE LITTLEFIELD: Do something like what?

SATAN: Number One: I'm not testifying at any more of these circle jerks no more—I'm not some wind-up doll to be summoned and dismissed like a fuckin' toy. Number Two: I want two souls before I leave here today—so take a memo, and pass it on upstairs. I'll take you and whoever.

JUDGE LITTLEFIELD: Me?

SATAN: Yeah, you. I shoulda claimed you off the dung heap after Lee's surrender . . . And I want some Darvon . . . And a tall bourbon neat.

(*To* CUNNINGHAM): What the fuck are you looking at?

CUNNINGHAM: I'd like to start my questioning.

SATAN: Why? You got some place you gotta be, dishrag?

CUNNINGHAM: No. When you're done crying, just let me know.

SATAN: Um, I'm sorry—maybe you can clear this up for me—but is today "Fuck-With-Someone-Who-Can-Rip-Your-Heart-Out-Through-Your-Miserable-Dried-Up-Cunt Day"? Is that what day this is? 'Cuz, unless I'm mistaken, I'm pretty sure that Today is not that Day.

CUNNINGHAM: Today is your day to answer my questions—when you're through behaving like a petulant child, that is.

JUDGE LITTLEFIELD: Cunningham! Cunningham, I am directing you to hit the off-switch on them flapping gums of yours until further notice! And you, Lou, with all due respect to your stature and station—could ya cut me a break here, please?!

SATAN: Frank, I've always been good to you—

JUDGE LITTLEFIELD: —and I to you—is that not so? Now lissen: Your complaint is duly noted and will be kicked upstairs at the conclusion of today's testimony, okay? Now I need to call the damn jury back in here. And what I need to know—from the both of youse—is that when I move to do so, that you two will conduct yourselves with a deportment in adjustment to the solemnity of these proceedings. Now, can I have your words on that?

CUNNINGHAM: I'm ready to proceed, Your Honor.

JUDGE LITTLEFIELD: With civility?

CUNNINGHAM: If I'm met with civility.

SATAN: You know what, Cunningham? All those excuses you got wedged between that dubious cleavage of yours: your mother, the bulimia, the herpes, the booze, the abortions, the rape, the bipolar pharmaceutical adventures, the twin suicide attempts and the abject failures at every relationship you ever attempted—all those things do nothing to Band-Aid the simple fact that There Comes a Time When the World Stops Rewarding Potential—and when that time came for you, you threw yourself the world's biggest pity party and dedicated the rest of your short, pathetic, inconsequential life to finding fault everywhere fuckin' else but in the return gaze of your own cosmetically altered reflection. Okay?

EL-FAYOUMY: Satan, please—you are perhaps out of bounds here!

SATAN: El-Fayoumy, on a good day, your cock measures three and a half inches erect and it goes off on a hair trigger if you so much as sneeze . . . Worse than that, you're a Flatterer, and your Love of God is utterly false—as is your hair color. And the sole reason you're so hot for this nasty train wreck over here is because you're addicted to tragedy and punishment—not because you *think* you're a piece of shit, but because, El-Fayoumy, the truth is: Your self-diagnosis is correct: You're a bag of hot air and a weakling—and you will never, ever, be loved.

( *To* CUNNINGHAM): You'll never be loved either, Cunningham, and that's because you're incapable of giving it—but you already knew that about yourself, didn't you?

(*To* JUDGE): You can bring in the jury now, Frank. Never let it be said that the Prince of Tyre stood in the way of Truth.

JUDGE LITTLEFIELD (*To* SATAN): No more outbursts.

SATAN: I'm a buddha floating on a lily pad.

JUDGE LITTLEFIELD (*Calling out*): El-Fayoumy—bring 'em on in!

EL-FAYOUMY: Uh . . . Sir, yes, sir, sir!

EL-FAYOUMY *opens door.* (*To jury*): Take your seats, please—Do not tarry.

*Jury enters.*

JUDGE LITTLEFIELD: Counselor, you may begin.

CUNNINGHAM: Mister Satan—

SATAN: I apologize for my earlier behavior, counselor—I had some bad fish at lunch.

CUNNINGHAM: Mister Satan, you've had a long-standing feud with God, correct?

SATAN: No. I love God.

CUNNINGHAM: You love God?

SATAN: Very much. God made me.

CUNNINGHAM: Okay, you say God made you—

SATAN: God did make me—it says so in the Bible.

CUNNINGHAM: I know about the Bible, Mister Satan. It also says in the Bible, in . . . in Matthew I believe. In Matthew, it, it says: "A good tree cannot bear bad fruit," correct?

SATAN: Correct.

CUNNINGHAM: So are you saying that you are good? Or are you saying that God is bad?

SATAN: I would never say that God is bad.

CUNNINGHAM: So, then, are you telling this court that you're good?

SATAN: I don't know—are you good, Counselor?

CUNNINGHAM: That's not what I asked you!

SATAN: I'm sorry.

CUNNINGHAM: Just answer the question.

SATAN: I don't believe in Good and Bad. What I believe in is Truth.

CUNNINGHAM: Fine. According to Job and Nehemiah, God created you in the first three days. True?

SATAN: True.

CUNNINGHAM: You were an "Angel."

SATAN: True.

CUNNINGHAM: You were present when God created Earth.

SATAN: True.

CUNNINGHAM: Then God created man and gave *him—not you*—dominion over the Earth. True?

SATAN: True.

CUNNINGHAM: You were, in fact, ordered by God to serve man. True?

SATAN: True.

CUNNINGHAM: According to Genesis and Ezekiel, you then tempted Eve to eat the Apple in order to prove to God that He had made an error in giving Man dominion over the Earth. At which point, according to Luke, you then "fell from Heaven like lightning" and became God's Adversary. And ever since that day, you have competed for Souls with God in order to try to prove the point that Man is not worthy to rule over the Earth. Isn't that true, Mister Satan?!

SATAN: I don't compete with God. God competes with himself.

CUNNINGHAM: That's not what I asked you.

SATAN: I'm trying to answer your question—

CUNNINGHAM: No, you are not trying to answer my question!

SATAN: Your Honor, I'm trying to form a response here—

JUDGE LITTLEFIELD: Let him answer, Cunningham!

EL-FAYOUMY: Your Honor, it does seem to me—

JUDGE LITTLEFIELD: Quiet! (*To* SATAN): Proceed.

SATAN: Thank you. Look, I didn't make you people, God did, okay? But there was a design flaw in the creation: He gave you Free Will—and to balance that out, you were designed to *Self-Correct*. But, unlike the "Free-Will" muscle, the "Self-Correct" muscle is not a particular favorite of the *Homo sapiens*. I'd say *"Self-Correct"* falls somewhere between "Colonoscopy" and "Firing Squad" on most people's holiday "wish" lists. At any rate, the truth is: I don't have to actively compete for human souls—I don't have to lull or flatter or tempt or deceive—because with God at the helm and you people running around wreaking havoc: I'll be honest, I spend most of my time on a sofa watching one-hour dramas on HBO.

CUNNINGHAM: And what? Getting tossed out of Heaven—that didn't bother you at all?

SATAN: There's a concept, Cunningham, called Playing the Cards You Are Dealt—One can either accept that concept or one can slowly lose one's mind, heart, and soul. I'd like to be more helpful to you here, but really, that's what it all comes down to.

CUNNINGHAM: Is that so?

SATAN: I'm just a fallen angel tryin' ta keep my dick hard in a monotheistic society—anything else you wanna ask?

CUNNINGHAM: Your Honor, this witness is clearly lying—I move that his entire testimony be stricken from the record.

JUDGE LITTLEFIELD: I'll not allow that, sorry—you conjured him, what comes out of his mouth is your responsibility.

CUNNINGHAM: But he's obviously lying!

SATAN: You oughta expand your consciousness, Counselor.

CUNNINGHAM: Your Honor!

JUDGE LITTLEFIELD: Unless you have another question, Cunningham, I suggest you step down now.

CUNNINGHAM: But—

JUDGE LITTLEFIELD: Forward or Back! You've been instructed, now what'll it be?

*A small beat.*

CUNNINGHAM: Why do you love God, Mister Satan?!

SATAN: What's not to love?

CUNNINGHAM: Specifically, Mister Satan! What specifically do you love about God?

SATAN: I don't know where to begin.

CUNNINGHAM: Pick a spot!

SATAN: I love God because He is All-Powerful and All-Forgiving. I love God because his Justice is perfect. I love God because God loves me.

CUNNINGHAM: God loves you?!

SATAN: Very much. Gift basket at Christmas—Hallmark Greetings on all the major holidays.

CUNNINGHAM: Stop it! If God loves you, then why did he throw you out of his Kingdom?!

SATAN: He didn't throw me out—I left.

CUNNINGHAM: That's not what it says in the Bible!

SATAN: Yeah, they fudged that part, you're right—but that's because you people really only respond to fear and threat—If they told you straight up that there was no lock to the Gates of Heaven, then you'd have no incentive at all to even try to be halfway decent.

CUNNINGHAM: In other words, God lied!

SATAN: God didn't write the Bible—you do know that, right?

CUNNINGHAM: Of course I know that!

SATAN: Then why would you say that God lied?

CUNNINGHAM: Mister Satan—does God love Judas Iscariot? Yes or No?!

SATAN: God loves everybody.

CUNNINGHAM: And yet Judas is in Hell—so what use is God's Love to Judas if my client is allowed to languish in Damnation?

SATAN: Your client is free to leave whenever he wants to—in fact, I wish he would—I could use the room.

CUNNINGHAM: That's not true and you know it!

SATAN: Look, maybe you should sit down and catch your breath—

CUNNINGHAM: —The real truth is that God's Love for us is Conditional—isn't that right?! You failed to meet God's conditions, and he threw you in the trash! Judas failed—and he's in a catatonic stupor!

SATAN: Your client succumbed to Despair—

CUNNINGHAM: Yes! And if Human Despair is so powerful as to render God powerless over it, then what does that say about God?! It says one of two things, Mister Satan: Either God's not All-Powerful and therefore useless—or—God's Love is Conditional, which renders that Love false and Unworthy! Which one is it?!

SATAN: Cunningham, please don't take this personally, but your father never really loved you or wanted you, right? And the only reason your mother didn't abort you was because she was afraid of scarring—I think she told you that once, didn't she—

CUNNINGHAM: Mister Satan!—

SATAN: —Just because your parents resented you doesn't mean that God does.

CUNNINGHAM: —Mister Satan, I asked you a direct question and I am demanding from you a direct answer!

SATAN: The direct answer is that you are completely wrong.

CUNNINGHAM: Is God Powerless or Spiteful—I am ordering you to answer!

SATAN (*not unkindly*): You're powerless and spiteful, Cunningham—not God.

CUNNINGHAM: Your Honor, he's not answering!

JUDGE LITTLEFIELD: Whaddya want me to do about it?

CUNNINGHAM: But he's not answering!

SATAN: Open your heart to God, Cunningham.

CUNNINGHAM: Shut up! (*To* JUDGE) Your Honor?!

JUDGE LITTLEFIELD: I suggest you step down, Cunningham.

CUNNINGHAM: But I'm not finished!

JUDGE LITTLEFIELD: Then finish!

CUNNINGHAM: But Your Honor, this isn't fair!

JUDGE LITTLEFIELD: It is what it is, Cunningham!

CUNNINGHAM: But Your Honor—

JUDGE LITTLEFIELD: Cunningham—

CUNNINGHAM: Your Honor—

JUDGE LITTLEFIELD: What, Cunningham? What?

*Pause.*

CUNNINGHAM (*To* SATAN): You're a fuckin' liar!!

SATAN: I'm truly sorry you feel that way.

*Pause.*

CUNNINGHAM: . . . . . . Nothing further.

JUDGE LITTLEFIELD: El-Fayoumy: Cross?

EL-FAYOUMY *surveys* CUNNINGHAM, *then* SATAN, *then back to* CUNNINGHAM.

EL-FAYOUMY: No cross. No.

JUDGE LITTLEFIELD: You're excused.

SATAN: Thanks, Frank.

(*To the lawyers*): Counselors: You availed yourselves as
expected. And by the way, El-Fayoumy, you're completely
wrong, too. I'll be in touch.

*And he is gone.*

JUDGE LITTLEFIELD: Next witness!

*Blackout. A beat.*

JESUS *makes his way to* JUDAS. *He speaks to us.*

JESUS: Right now, I am in Fallujah. I am in Darfur. I am on
Sixty-third and Park having dinner with Ellen Barkin and
Ron Perelman . . . Right now, I'm on Lafayette and Astor
waiting to hit you up for change so I can get high. I'm
taking a walk through the Rose Garden with George Bush.
I'm helping Donald Rumsfeld get a good night's sleep . . . I
was in that cave with Osama, and on that plane with
Mohamed Atta . . . And what I want you to *know* is that
your work has barely begun. And what I want you to *trust* is
the efficacy of divine love if practiced consciously. And what
I need you to *believe* is that if you hate who I love, you do
not know me at all. And make no mistake, "Who I Love" is
every last one. I *am* every last one. People ask of me: Where
are you? Where are you? . . . Verily I ask of you to ask
yourself: Where are *you?* Where are *you?*
   Judas.

*No response.*

   Judas.

*Beat.* JUDAS *slowly emerges from his frozen state of catatonia.*

JUDAS: . . . . . . Who's that?
JESUS: Is it ever anybody else, Judas?

*Pause.*

    I miss you.
JUDAS: Uh-huh.
JESUS: I miss you, Judas.

JESUS *lays a hand on him.*

JUDAS: *DON'T FUCKIN' TOUCH ME!*
JESUS: Judas.
JUDAS: *I SAID TAKE YOUR FUCKIN' HANDS OFF ME—
    TAKE 'EM OFF!*
JESUS: I'm sorry. I'm—
JUDAS: *—JUST BACK OFF MY GRILL, MAN! BACK OFF!*
JESUS: I'm sorry.
JUDAS: *BACK OFF MORE!*
JESUS: I'm sorry.

*Pause.*

    Judas: If a thousand strangers spit on me and kick me as
    they pass, I will smile. But if the brother of my heart gives me
    only a passing hard look, then, Judas—I will not sleep that
    night, nor sleep—at all—till he will let me love him again.
JUDAS: *NO!!*
JESUS: No, what?
JUDAS: No more fuckin' fortune cookies, that's what! You
    wanna say something, I can't stop you—you wanna

apologize, fine, apologize and go, just—for once—speak like
a normal fuckin' person!

JESUS: I'm not a normal person, Judas, and I'm not here to
apologize. I am who I am and not what you demand me to
be. I'm always going to be who I am and what I am, and
when have you ever heard me deliver my message any
differently, Judas? When?

JUDAS: I . . . Just, go away.

JESUS: I won't go away.

JUDAS: Well, that'd be a first.

JESUS: I have never gone away, Judas . . . Look at me.

JUDAS *does.*

I love you, Judas. And all I want—all I want—is to be not
just near you—but *with* you.

JUDAS: Shoulda thought of that before.

JESUS: Before what?

JUDAS: Just get the fuck outta here, okay?

JESUS: Judas—

JUDAS: Don't fuckin' Judas me—*You're not wanted here,* okay,
Mister Fuckin'-Above-It-All?!

JESUS: I'm not above it all—I'm right here in it, don't you see
that?

JUDAS: *And don't you get that I don't fuckin' care?!*

JESUS: You think your suffering is a one-way street?! It's not!
It's the exact opposite of not!

JUDAS: You got a lot of fuckin' nerve—

JESUS: —and you've got no nerve at all! Where's your *heart* in
all this, Judas? You think you were with me for any other
reason than that?! It was your heart, Judas. You were *all
heart.* You were my heart! Don't you know that?!

JUDAS: I'll tell you what I know: I watched you trip over your own dusty feet to heal the sick, the blind, the lame, the unclean—*any two-bit stranger stubbed their fuckin' toe!* When some lowly distant relative—too cheap to buy enough wine for his own fuckin' wedding—suddenly runs out of booze—no problem, you just "presto change-o"— *and it was fuckin' Miller time in ol' Canaan again, wasn't it, bro?! But when I fuckin' needed you—where the fuck were you, huh?!*

JESUS: Judas—

JUDAS: You forgave Peter and bullshit Thomas—you knocked Paul of Tarsus off a horse—you raised Lazarus from the *fuckin' dead*—but me? Me? Your "heart"? . . . *What about me??!! What about me, Jesus?! Huh?!* You just, you just—I made a mistake! And if that was wrong, then you should have told me! And if a broken heart wasn't sufficient reason to hang, *THEN YOU SHOULD HAVE TOLD ME THAT, TOO!*

JESUS: Don't you think . . . that if I knew that it would have changed your mind . . . that I would have?

*Pause.*

JUDAS: All I know is that you broke me unfixable—and that I'm here . . . And, you wanna know when you delivered your message differently? At the Temple, Jesus—that's when. And you were beautiful there. And you left there three inches taller. And we all saw it. I loved you. That's all I did. And that's the truth. And now I'm here.

JESUS: Judas—What if I were to tell you that you are not here? That you are with me in my Kingdom even now, and that you have been there since the morning of my Ascension and that you have never left?

JUDAS *spits in* JESUS*'s face.*

JUDAS: That's what I think about you.

JESUS *doesn't wipe it off.*

JESUS: I love you, Judas.

*Pause.*

I love you.

JUDAS: *Just stop!*

JESUS: Don't you see me here, Judas?

JUDAS: *I see a lot of things!*

JESUS: You see alotta things?

JUDAS: *That's right!*

JESUS: How about him? Do you see him?

SATAN *appears.*

Do you know him? Call unto him. Touch him. He is not there. Because he does not exist, Judas. Rather, they must conjure him, and still he is but a vapor blown away by a hummingbird's breath. He is false. He is a lie. He is not real. Touch him. Go ahead.

JUDAS: I don't wanna touch him.

JESUS: Stand up, Judas.

JUDAS: You know I can't do that!

JESUS: No. What I know—is that you can.

JUDAS: Get the fuck over yourself!

JESUS: Will you feed my lambs, Judas? . . . Will you take care of my little sheep? . . . Will you feed my lambs?!

JUDAS: "Feed your lambs"?

JESUS: You know exactly what I'm asking you.

JUDAS: Go away!

JESUS: If you don't love me, Judas—then you're gonna have to look me in my eyes and say it.

JUDAS: I don't love you.

JESUS: If you don't love me, then why are you here?

JUDAS: Go!

JESUS: Judas! . . . Judas, don't you know what would happen the very instant you got down on your knees?

JUDAS: Why on my knees? They shoulda buried me standing up—'cuz I been on my knees my whole life! You left me.

JUDAS *is slowly reverting to his frozen catatonic state.*

JESUS: I'm right here.

JUDAS: I would have never believed that you could have left me.

JESUS: I never left you.

JUDAS: That you didn't love me.

JESUS: I do love you.

JUDAS: Why . . . didn't you make me good enough . . . so that you could've loved me?

JESUS: . . . Please take my hands, Judas. Please.

JUDAS: Where are they?

JESUS: Right here.

JUDAS: I can't see them.

JESUS: They're right here.

JUDAS: *Where are you going?!*

JESUS: I'm right here.

JUDAS: *Don't leave me!*

JESUS: I'm here.

JUDAS: I can't hurt . . .

JESUS: I love you, Judas.

JUDAS: I can't . . .

JESUS: Please stay.

STEPHEN ADLY GUIRGIS

JUDAS: I can't hurt . . .

JESUS: Please love me, Judas.

JUDAS: I can't.

JUDAS *is frozen again.*

*A long beat.*

BUTCH HONEYWELL *enters* JUDAS*'s lair with a twelve-pack of Canadian beer.* BUTCH *looks around, clears his throat, takes off his cap.*

BUTCH HONEYWELL: Um, uh, Mister Iscariot? Uh, Mister Iscariot, I, uh, I don't know if you can hear me, but, I just— I just wanted to introduce myself, if, if I could. I'm, uh, Butch Honeywell. I was the foreman of the jury at your trial there . . . and . . . well, we found you guilty, Mister Iscariot . . . I'm real sorry about that . . . Oh, uh . . . I brought you a twelve-pack of beer. Actually, guess it's a five-pack now, but, anyway . . . Here. I don't know if you drink beer, but it's good stuff . . . Anyways, I'll just set it down right beside you right here . . . Okay then.

BUTCH *goes to leave, then stops.*

. . . So . . . I think I'm dead, Mister Iscariot, and, I'm a little concerned about that 'cuz I don't think my soul's ready for judgment, but nobody else has so far corroborated that I'm dead so, I just don't bring it up, but, the fact is that if this is a dream, it's the longest damn dream I've ever endured—and really, I just . . . I really miss my wife, Mister Iscariot. Is it okay if I tell you that?

*Beat.* BUTCH *pops a beer. Sips. Pause.*

I remember, I was with these two girls that night, when I first seent my wife, Mister Iscariot. It was a party at Jimmy Rayburn's house 'cuz Jimmy's momma worked till midnight so he had the house to himself, and, you know, me and these two girls—Suzie Heller and Della Mae Robbins—we were just talkin', smokin' cigarettes, out on Mrs. Rayburn's deck away from the party. I was depressed over sumpthin' or other—prolly 'cuz school was ending—plus I had just been in the school play—I had played Tom in *The Glass Menagerie*—it was the first time I had ever acted, and everyone said I was real good. But now, the play was over, and school was almost over, and, for the part in the play, they had given me this real short haircut—like 1940s style— and my ears, Mister Iscariot, I don't know if you can notice, but, they stick out a little bit, so, with the short haircut and all, I was feeling a little self-conscious and dumb, and, anyway, just not too cheery . . . So anyways, I'm out there on the deck talkin' to Suzie and Della—and all a the sudden I see this girl inside at the party. She had, I guess, just arrived, and she had on a red jacket. It was a cheerleading jacket from the high school just across the state line in Virginia—The Red Raiders—and I remember, all I saw was blonde hair, and a red jacket, and this smile that was—even from a distance—just kinda electrifying to the heart, ya know? 'Bout a minute later, the sliding door to the deck opens, and this girl, she comes out by herself, and she's heading towards us—turns out she's friends with Della from back in the day, from, I don't know, Girl Scouts, Brownies, sumpthin' like that. Anyways, she walks over—and she was so beautiful, that I remember thinkin' to myself—and this is exactly word for word what I thought—"I ain't even gonna bother talkin' to this girl." So she comes over, says hello, and I just excuse myself right off the deck and head back inside,

STEPHEN ADLY GUIRGIS

fixin' ta say my "good-byes" and skedaddle . . . And
anyways, I try to leave, but then, Jimmy handed me a beer,
and someone else started passin' a bottle of Rebel Yell, and
before you know it, you know, bong hits and whatnot, and
anyways a little later I'm sittin' on the couch when this girl—
my future wife—she just comes up to me by herself and she
says: "I saw you in that play the other night. You made me
cry" . . . Two days later, we went out on a date . . . On the
way back, I was driving her home, and we passed by this
house where my friend Dave Hoghe used to live who had
died . . . I hadn't been by his house since he passed. The
family didn't live there no more. But when I saw the house,
I got struck with this feeling, and I asked her if she wouldn't
mind if we just pulled up in front of that house and just sat
for a moment. She said: "Sure." So I parked, and we just sat
in the car for a while. Quiet. Not sayin' nothin'. And before
I knew it, Mister Iscariot, I was tearing up—'cuz this kid, he
had been a real good friend of mine, ya know—and then, I
just started crying, Mister Iscariot. I couldn't help myself
and I couldn't shut it off. And I was real embarrassed, and
she just, she just held me while tears and snot and whatnot
just poured outta me and onto her little white sweater . . .
And she didn't mind about that . . . She didn't mind at
all . . . At some point, I drove her home, and we got to her
door, and we started to kiss, and, well, God, it was like, I'll
tell ya—it was like peaches and dynamite . . . And before I
left, I apologized to her about the crying and all, and she
said: "Don't be a jackass, Butch Honeywell," and I smiled,
but then I went on to explain my meaning, which was—you
know—if you want a girl to think you're sensitive or
something, then maybe taking her to the house of your
dead friend and crying all over her pretty white sweater
might be a good way to pull it off, and, you know what

she said, Mister Iscariot? . . . She looked at me for a good long while with them all the way dazzling eyes of hers and then she just said: "Well, if it was a trick . . . then I'm tricked" . . . . . . . . . . Three years into our marriage, I took a job teaching at the State College—I was popular with the students 'cuz I found a way to make 'em wanna learn. One night, at the end of the semester, they took me out for beers. I ended up havin' an assignation with one of the coeds— young lady named Lucy. And I went home that night, got into bed next to my wife drunk as a skunk and I remember, before I passed out, I was lookin' at her. I always liked to look at her when she was sleeping 'cuz she always looked so good. I had a little nickname for her, I useta call her "my little baby dinosaur," 'cuz that's how she looked like when she slept—like one of those cute cartoon little baby dinosaurs—like a little brontosaurus, but cute . . . Anyways, when I woke up the next mornin', she was still sleepin', and what I had done the night before came back to me, and I looked at my wife, and, boy, she looked exactly the same as always, but, somehow, she just wasn't my little baby dinosaur no more, ya know? And she woke up, and she didn't know nuthin' 'bout nuthin', and everything was exactly the same as if the night before had never happened, except, it wasn't the same, and I knew it. And I had no idea why I had done what I done. But I had done it. And it couldn't be changed. My girl, she got up and fixed blueberry French toast with maple walnut pecans. I didn't eat it. No way I coulda eaten it. Nuthin' was ever the same after that morning, Mister Iscariot, ya know? I tried a lot of things to make it better, the only thing that did was more beer and women . . . Do you know who W. H. Auden was, Mister Iscariot? W. H. Auden was a poet who once said: "God may reduce you on Judgement Day to tears of shame, reciting by

STEPHEN ADLY GUIRGIS

heart the poems you would have written, had your life been good" . . . She was my poem, Mister Iscariot. Her and the kids. But mostly . . . her . . . You cashed in Silver, Mister Iscariot, but me? Me, I threw away Gold . . . That's a fact. That's a natural fact.

*A long beat.*

JESUS *sighs, takes off his shirt, plunges it in the bucket, rinses it, and begins to wash* JUDAS*'s feet.* JESUS *washes meticulously and with care. He washes. And washes. Perhaps the water is mixed with tears.*

*Lights fade.*

*The end*

# Acknowledgments

Much Grateful Thanks Firstly to the Following: The
LAByrinth Theater Company, George C. Wolfe, Mara Manus,
Michael Hurst, Peter Dubois, Irene Cabrera, Celise Kalke,
Steven Showalter, Jordan Thaler, Heidi Griffiths, Kenneth
Leslie and all the ushers and staff at The Public Theater;
Marieke Gaboury, Sallie D. Sanders, Amanda Woods, Abby
Marcus, Veronica R. Bainbridge, Monique Carboni, Brian
Roff, Michael Almereyda, Terrence Morris, Robin L. Cook,
John Concado, Courtney Wetzel, Ashley Hanna, Florencia
Lozano, Chris Rubino, Monica Moore, Maddalena Deichman,
Andromache Chalfant, Mimi O'Donnell, Japhy Weideman,
Darron L. West, Madonna Badger, Kimberly Braswell, Colin
Calender, David Deblinger, Michael J. Fine, Lulie Haddad,
Ruth Hendl, Jeffrey A. Horwitz, Margo Lion, John Marcus,
Ricardo E. Oquendo, Daryl Roth, John Gould Rubin, Carlo
Alban, Simone Allmen, Vanessa Aspillaga, Liche Ariza, Dick
Benedek, Maggie Bofill, John Buzzetti, Elizabeth Canavan,
Andrea Ciannavei, Rebecca Cohen, Beth Cole, Alexis
Croucher, Billy Crudup, Kim Director, Faber and Faber, Rev.
Dr. James A. Forbes Jr. of the Riverside Church, the Gersh
Agency, Bob Glaudini, Charles Goforth, Robyn Goodman,
Marie Therese Guirgis, Maurice and Therese Guirgis, Mark
Hammer, HBO Films, Ron Cephas Jones, Jen Konawal, Diane
Landers, Brett C. Leonard, Trevor Long, MCC Playwrights'

Coalition, Chris McGarry, Sara Murphy, New River Dramatists and Mark Woods and Meir Ribalow and Big Bill Baker in Healing Springs, North Carolina, Dierdre O'Connell, Ana Ortiz, Sarah Almond, Denise Oswald, Richie Petrocelli, Michael Pitt, Ira Pittelman, Portia, Father Raymond Rafferty of Corpus Christi Church, Joselin Reyes, Nancy Rose and Ira Shreck, Brendan Sexton, John Patrick Shanley, Marshall Sharer, Jamey Sheridan, Todd Solondz, Erana Stennett, Arielle Tepper, Sister Mary Tyler O.P., Sam Wilsche, David Zayas, and Emily Ziff.

Secondly: I can't even imagine what writing this play would have been like without the theological advice and spiritual guidance of Father Jim Martin, S.J. My mom always says that back in the day, Priests were Men of God who were Our Friends. Father Jim was exactly that. His knowledge, enthusiasm, and gentle caring was essential not only to my writing process, but to the rehearsals and the production as well. Father Jim is a real priest, a real man, and the Real Deal.

Thirdly: Philip Seymour Hoffman. Incredible director. Trusted collaborator. Treasured friend.

Fourthly: John Ortiz. The other blessing of my creative life. His confidence and faith in me since we were kids is a debt I can never repay. All heart. Gigantic.

Fifthly: The Original Cast. Sam Rockwell and Yul Vázquez committed to the play before there was a script and never hedged. Liza Colón-Zayas, Elizabeth Rodriguez, Yetta Gottesman, and Craig "Mums" Grant committed on, like, page 9. Eric Bogosian signed on at about page 20. Jeffrey DeMunn took a leap of faith and said yes based on a reading (page 50?) and a phone call. The great Adrian Martinez endured an audition, even though we had already worked together once before. John Ortiz stayed in town—and in debt—to play Jesus, even when Jesus had no lines. Salvatore

Inzerillo asked me if he'd at least get to play a part "with some meat on the bone." I said: "Probably not." Sal said yes anyway. Stephen McKinley Henderson was the steal of the draft. Deborah Rush and Kohl Sudduth gave incredible auditions and then said yes to supporting and still developing roles in an unfinished script. Callie Thorne was the last actor we saw, just a few days before the first rehearsal. I can't really remember her audition, but I'll never forget her performance and her commitment. I can never ever thank these actors enough. They were all unique and beautiful, fierce, committed, talented, willing, and generous. Truly.

Lastly and most important: God. I struggle with God. I struggle with Life. I want simple answers and easy solutions. I want to do it on my own and always be in control. Mostly, I want to avoid the uncomfortable, which only leads to more discomfort. God is, I think, perhaps, The Unavoidable, and writing, for me, is the curse that brings me a little bit closer to that Unavoidable entity that ultimately allows me freedom and access to my work and to my life. Some people are curious about a writer's "creative process." I can't explain mine except to say that God is the starting point and the finish line. In other words, when all else fails—and it always does—I pray.